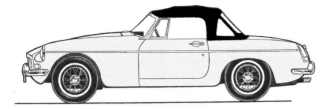

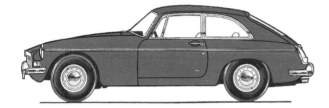

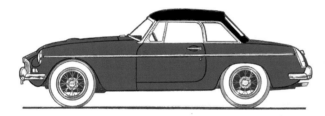

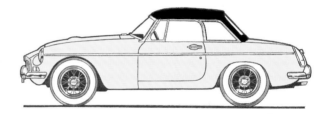

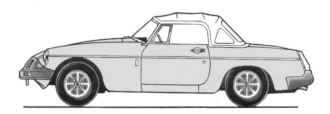

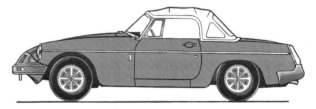

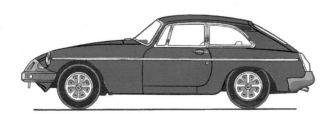

MGB

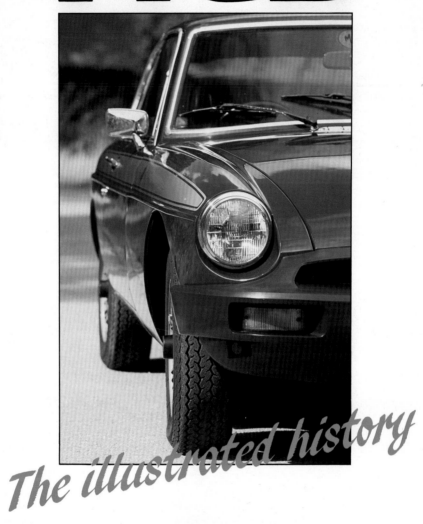

The illustrated history

Jonathan Wood & Lionel Burrell

Foulis

Haynes

National colours: red, white and blue MGs,
left to right, MGC, MGB GT V8 and MGB.

First published 1988
Reprinted 1989
Second edition 1993
Reprinted 1994, 1996 and 1999

G. T. Foulis & Company is an imprint of
Haynes Publishing,
Sparkford, Nr. Yeovil, Somerset
BA22 7JJ, England

Tel. 01963 440635 Fax: 01963 440001
Int. tel: +44 1963 440635 Fax: +44 1963 440001
E-mail: sales@haynes-manuals.co.uk
Web site: http://www.haynes.com

Haynes North America, Inc.
861 Lawrence Drive, Newbury Park,
California 91320 USA

British Library Cataloguing in Publication Data
Wood, Jonathan
MGB
1. MGB cars
I. Title   II. Burrell, Lionel
629.2'222
ISBN 0-85429-948-3

Library of Congress catalog card number 93-79172

Printed in England by J. H. Haynes & Co. Ltd.

Safety Fast!

Contents

Introduction to the Second Edition

WHEN THIS book was published in 1988, the MGB had been out of production for eight years and it would have been fanciful to suggest that it had any chance of revival. Yet in April 1993, the first example of its spiritual successor, the MG RV8, left its Cowley assembly line, and with it has come the rebirth of the MG marque. The seeds of its revival are enshrined in the British Motor Heritage MGB bodyshell, which appeared in 1988, and was also featured in the first edition of this book.

It would not have been possible to chart the extraordinary revival in the marque's fortunes without the assistance of the Rover Group, and I owe a particular debt of gratitude to Michael Kennedy, its director of external affairs and also to press officer Kevin Jones. Thanks are due to Stephen Schlemmer, director of Rover Special Products at Gaydon, to MG RV8 project director Graham Irvine at Cowley, and to manufacturing manager Cliff Law, while Mark Gamble provided much useful detail on the RV8's evolution.

There would never have been an MG RV8 if it had not been for British Motor Heritage and the energies of executive director David Bishop. I am grateful to him for sharing his memories, and to manufacturing manager at Faringdon Jack Bellinger, and his successor David Bloomfield. Valuable assistance was rendered by John Brigden of Brigden Coulter PR.

If the appearance of the MG RV8 is a tribute to a single individual, it is to MG's former chief engineer Syd Enever, creator of the MGB. He died on 9 February 1993 at the age of 86, and in the following year, on 15 July 1994, John Thornley who with Enever conceived the B, died aged 85.

Jonathan Wood
Frensham, Surrey

Introduction to the First Edition

THIS BOOK could not have been written without a considerable amount of help and, first and foremost, my thanks must go to John Thornley, MGs general manager from 1952 to 1969, who gave the project his wholehearted support. I am enormously grateful for the help and advice he gave me and also for contributing the Foreword.

One January afternoon, John played host to all the key personalities in the MGB project. MG's last three chief engineers were present: Syd Enever, who retired in 1971, his successor Roy Brocklehurst and Don Hayter who took over from him in 1973. Also Henry Stone, development department foreman, contributed important points of detail. For a few hours the famous 'Abingdon spirit' was rekindled, the conversation being preserved on my tape recorder. Both Roy, who was responsible for detailing the MGB's mechanical layout and Don, who styled the car, also granted me lengthy interviews, so the following account of the MGB's history is largely based on first-hand recollections.

Thanks are also due to Doug Gardner, production and plant engineering manager, for providing important dates and details.

I am also indebted to R.A. Burden, Austin Rover's external affairs planning manager and to Anders Clausager, archivist of the British Motor Industry Heritage Trust, who offered every assistance and not only undertook the time consuming job of tracking down the vast majority of photographs used in this book, which are courtesy of the Rover Group plc, unless otherwise stated, but also compiled the 1962 MGB production table.

John Seager, Installation and Services Engineer at Abingdon, kindly lent me some of the photographs he prudently took during the last weeks of the factory's existence in October 1980.

Thanks are due to Neill Bruce, who wielded his camera with his customary skill and was responsible for the colour photographs of the 1967 MGB roadster, MGC and MGB GT V8.

I am also grateful to MG enthusiasts who loaned their cars for photography. They are MGB owners Roger Jerram (1967 roadster), Danny Waters (1977 American specification roadster). Geoff Simpson (1980 Limited Edition roadster), Bernard Rengger (1967 GT), Brian Holland (1980 GT) and Mike Akers (1964 MGB Berlinette 1800). Also my thanks to Roger Mace (MGC) and Phil Edwards (MG GT V8).

Whether you're a past or present MG owner, or just like motor cars, I trust that you'll be fascinated and maybe a little saddened by what follows.

Jonathan Wood
Frensham, Surrey

Author's note

I have Lionel Burrell, associate editor of *Classic Cars* magazine, to thank for providing not only the idea for this book, but for also producing the magnificent coloured fold out illustrations of the MGB, MGC and MGB GT V8, which first appeared in black and white form in *Autocar* magazine and are reproduced by kind permission of Reed Business Publishing's Quadrant Picture Library. I am also grateful to Bob Murray, editor of *Autocar* and Howard Walker, editor of *Motor* for permission to quote brief extracts from their road tests of the MGB, MGC and MGB GT V8.

While this book was going to press, I was saddened to hear of the sudden death, following a stroke, on 29 April 1988, of 55-year-old Roy Brocklehurst, who played a key role in the MGB's creation, and whose words so enliven this text. *J.W.*

Foreword

by John Thornley, OBE,
General Manager, MG Car
Company, 1952-1969

THIS BOOK IS more than a history of the MGB; it is a tribute to its designer, man of genius Albert Sydney Enever. It is not correct to describe him as an untrained engineer because he trained himself; he had an insatiable curiosity about why things happened, a curiosity which went far beyond purely engineering and automotive matters, so that he had knowledge of a wide variety of subjects which would hold one spellbound – if only one could get him talking. By nature he is a quiet man – except when something stings him – and it is because of this taciturnity that he was not more widely recognised in his heyday. But maybe it is never too late so that, by this book, Jonathan Wood has brought him some of the acclaim that is his due.

Prior to the MGB, Sydney had had his hand in several vehicles of which those to make greatest claim on the automotive headlines were the MGA and the record-breaking EX 181. It was on this latter that he drew for the shape of the MGB which was, moreover, his first assay into monocoque. And he got it right: so right that, although the car was intended for a production life of the customary five years or so, circumstances dictated that it went on and on, and was still outselling its competitors eighteen years later.

When Sydney retired, others took on the battle to keep the MGB abreast of the ever more complex construction and use regulations. This book tells of Roy Brocklehurst, Don Hayter, Terry Mitchell, Jim O'Neill and the rest who carried on the good work and all of whom, I know, feel that they owe at least as much to Sydney as I do.

John Thornley

Creator of the MGB
Albert Sydney (Syd) Enever,
Chief engineer, the MG Car Company,
1954-1971.

Chapter I

Abingdon and the birth of the MGB

THE MGB is not only the most successful MG ever built, in its heyday it was the world's top selling high-performance car with over half a million examples produced between 1962 and 1980. By far and away the most popular British car to be sold in America since the war, the MGB was, it should be remembered, not one model but two: a stylish, practical, well mannered 100 mph roadster for the enthusiast, with an enviable sporting pedigree; and a closed GT derivative, possessing many of the advantages of its open stablemate, but able to double as a family car if necessary. Arguably, too, it was one of the best looking British cars of the 1960s.

The MGB was the product of imaginative management, a talented and enthusiastic engineering team and is a fitting tribute to the abilities of Sydney Enever, MG's outstanding chief engineer. Its tragedy was that the car's 18 year production span coincided with the most turbulent era in the British motor industry's history and it survived no less than three corporate upheavals. MG's strength, and weakness, has always been its dependence on the switchback financial fortunes of its corporate parent.

Despite the popularity of the MG name amongst members of the public, over the years the firm's Cowley-, Longbridge- and London-based masters have often displayed indifference, incomprehension and even downright hostility to the extraordinary chemistry that was Abingdon. The fact that MG, along with Rover and Jaguar, will probably be one of the mainstream British motoring marque names to survive into the 21st century is in no small part due to the MGB possessing that indefinable 'Abingdon

Touch' which was reflected by its surviving 10 years longer than its projected manufacturing life in a decade of lacklustre and now largely forgotten models.

Announced in 1962, when the British Motor Corporation was outwardly riding high, the MGB was due for replacement by 1970. But in 1968, BMC was absorbed, with governmental encouragement, into the British Leyland Motor Corporation. Then, in 1975, came nationalisation and the creation of Leyland Cars, the year in which the previous administration's Triumph TR7 corporate sports car made its appearance, an event which could only spell death in the long term for the superior, but ageing, MGB. In 1978 came yet another restructuring and the creation of BL Cars. Although the long running MGB still enjoyed a loyal following on both sides of the Atlantic, in 1979 the soaring value of the pound wrought havoc with the model's all important American sales. With no suitable replacement, MGB production ceased in 1980 and with it went the Abingdon factory that had been the MG Car Company's home for 51 years.

To see how the MGB possessed such a pedigree, we must briefly return to the Oxford of the early 1920s which was where the MG car was born. The creator and instigator of the marque was Cecil Kimber (1888-1945), an engineer and enthusiast with a receptive eye for line and proportion who, in 1921, had joined the Oxford based Morris Garages as sales manager. This establishment was the original retail arm of William Morris's car manufacturing empire which, not suprisingly, held the Oxford agency for Morris cars. In March 1922, Kimber became general manager and, in the

Something special: this handsome aluminium-bodied Morris Oxford produced by Morris Garages, was of the type marketed as the 'M.G. Special 4-seater Sports' from April 1924. The car followed one produced for G.S. 'Jack' Gardiner, a Morris Garages salesman, which was delivered to him in March 1924. Trials driver Billy Cooper ordered a similar car, completed in May, and this might have been the fourth, which was photographed in June 1924. Although still badged a Morris Oxford, this special-bodied 14/28 Morris was the first of its type also to carry the famous MG octagonal badge. This car is not fitted with front wheel brakes; note the speedometer drive on the nearside front wheel. Like Cooper's car it was fitted with wheel discs to disguise the utilitarian artilleries; that of the spare can be seen reflected in the body side. The stork mascot is in the manner of that used by Hispano-Suiza.

following year, he took the initiative and produced a special-bodied Bullnose Morris: the Morris Garages Chummy, an up market variation on the utilitarian Cowley theme. Nineteen-twenty-four saw the effective birth of the MG (for Morris Garages) marque with the arrival of its famous octagonal badge, executed in what we now call the Art Deco style and the work of Ted Lee, Kimber's cost accountant, who was also a keen amateur artist. Initially it played second fiddle to the Morris badge and appeared below it on the radiator proper but, from late 1927, it displaced the Morris emblem and has appeared on every MG since then.

MG's history is punctuated by a series of significant milestones and the year of 1928 marked a turning point in the firm's affairs. That year the MG Car Company was established and demand for Kimber's products meant that the cars were produced, from 1927, at a purpose built factory in Edmund Road, Oxford. Then, in the late summer of 1928, came the 18/80, a good looking, though

13

MGB
The illustrated history

expensive fast tourer, with a purpose-designed chassis and 2.4 litre six-cylinder overhead camshaft engine, shared with the Morris Isis. Significantly, it was fitted not with the usual Morris radiator but a new one, a distinctive rectangular rendering designed by Kimber himself and destined, in essence, to feature on every road going MG until 1955. It was followed, in the same year, by the £175 Midget, the first popular MG; its sophisticated overhead camshaft engine hailed from Wolseley, Morris having purchased the firm in 1927. This distinctive configuration was to power every MG car until 1935.

As demand for MGs increased, space again became a problem, so Kimber began to look around for new premises. He eventually found them, not in the city, but six miles away in the Thames-side town of Abingdon. There, on the Marcham Road, just to the west of the town, was a disused factory adjoining the premises of the Pavlova Leather Company, which had been used for the manufacture of leather coats for troops during the

MG's Abingdon factory, its home from 1929 until 1980, pictured in 1964, two years after the MGB's introduction. The Marcham Road is in the foreground with the original factory, known as A Block after the war, on the right and Abingdon General Hospital on the left fronting the road. A Block housed the production lines, the MGBs being assembled there. B Block opposite was built as separate structures during the Second World War, with the gaps between them filled in as they were required, and contained the competition department and rectification section with design and development housed in the end bay, with the boiler house beyond. The export compound can be seen above and to the left of B Block. After this photograph was taken in 1965, C Block was built to house the transport and competition departments, along with the stores. The original Pavlova Leather Works can be seen on the right, above A Block. The company still occupies the site.

First World War. Morris Garages was already using it for storing stocks of used cars and the firm moved there in September 1929. It was to be MG's home for more than half a century.

The marque's sporting pedigree was honed during the 1930 to 1935 era and the most significant model, as far as our story is concerned, was the two-seater J2 of 1932. Its functional lines, humped twin scuttles, cutaway doors and exposed petrol tank represented for many the quintessence of the British pre-war sports car, a formula that, incredibly, endured until 1955. In addition to sports car sales, Kimber also produced racing cars, which were sold to private owners, and did wonders for the marque's reputation. Despite successes on the race track, however, production dropped from a peak of 2400 cars built in 1932 to 1200 in 1935. With a growing model diversification, MGs were becoming progressively divorced from their Morris parentage.

In the meantime, the affairs of Morris Motors had drifted, the model range became unwieldy, and in 1933 and 1934 the rival Austin company built more cars. Morris responded by bringing in the dynamic Leonard Lord, who had started his career with Morris Engines at Coventry. Lord embarked on a policy of rationalistation. A drastic, and much needed, re-investment programme was initiated at Cowley and, in 1934, Lord launched the Morris Eight which was destined to be the best selling British car of the nineteen thirties.

It was not long before Lord began taking a critical look at the companies, and MG was one, which remained the personal property of Lord Nuffield, as Morris became in 1934. As a result, on 1 July 1935, the MG Car Company, along with Wolseley, was sold to Morris Motors. Out went the racing programme, the Abingdon drawing office was closed and design responsibility for MG cars was transferred to Cowley. Wolseley and MG thereafter produced models with cheaper pushrod engines, which although less potent than their overhead camshaft predecessors, were easier to maintain. This new approach was typified by the arrival of the new SA sports saloon in 1936 intended as Morris Motors' response to the growing popularity of William Lyons' new and successful SS marque. However, sports car production was maintained with the TA of 1936, visually similar to its predecessors, but

powered by a 1.3 litre pushrod engine of Wolseley 10 ancestry. It evolved into the almost identical 1.2 litre TB of 1939, though it used a new engine which powered all MG's sports cars until 1955. This EXPAG unit was derived from the 1.1 litre four produced for the 1938 Morris 10, and enlarged to 1.2 litres when used by MG.

The delightful MG TB Midget of 1939 was essentially the same as its TA predecessor, with the exception of its engine, which was to power every MG car until 1955. Under the bonnet was the new 1.2 litre overhead valve XPAG engine, of Morris ancestry, which had appeared in 1.1 litre form in the Series M Morris 10, announced in the previous autumn. With it came a new gearbox, with synchromesh on top and third gears, while synchromesh on second was a first for an MG sports car! The TB formed the basis of the post-war TC, which appeared in 1945 ...

... and was virtually identical to its pre-war predecessor, with the exception of the beloved sliding trunnion rear suspension, introduced on the C-type Midget of 1931, and discarded in favour of these more conventional shackles. The charming two-seater body was also four inches wider than the TB's. The TC sold a then record 10,000 examples between 1945 and 1949 and paved the way for the more successful TD of 1950. As the British government was directing car companies to export their products overseas, the TC became the first MG to sell in quantity to America, with 2001 examples, or 20 per cent total production, being so designated. However, the TD sold even better in the US, with 23,488 of the 29,664 built finding American owners, so paving the way for the TF, MGA and, finally, the MGB.

With the outbreak of the Second World War in 1939, MG was firmly established as a marque, along with Morris, Wolseley and Riley, within the Nuffield umbrella and Abingdon had the distinction of being the largest sports car factory in the world. About 22,500 MGs had been built since the marque's faltering beginnings in 1924. MG car production ceased during hostilities but these war years were clouded by the sudden departure of Cecil Kimber in November 1941. He had been summarily dismissed by Miles Thomas, Nuffield's new

vice chairman and managing director, on the grounds that he had obtained a contract for the front section of the Albemarle bomber (Abingdon eventually built 635 of them) and such an initiative was not in step with centralised corporate policy. Kimber subsequently joined the Charlesworth coachbuilding concern to reorganise its plant for aircraft production. He then moved to Specialloid Pistons as works director. Cecil Kimber died tragically in a railway accident outside Kings Cross Station in February 1945, just three months before the European war ended. He was only 56 years old.

With Kimber gone, George Propert, formerly works manager, took over as general manager, while Harold Ryder, a Morris director since 1926, was given responsibility for MG at Cowley. Car production restarted in October 1945 with the TC

sports two-seater, a mildly updated pre-war TB, while in 1947 came the Y Type saloon, with independent front suspension, held over from 1939. The accent was on exports as a buoyant balance of payments position was a central plank of Clement Attlee's post-war Labour government. Hitherto, MGs had been closely geared to the needs of the home market but, by the late 1940s, they were being exported as far afield as Australia and America though not as many to the latter country as legend suggests. Nevertheless, the TC's impact was enormous and paved the way for the similarly traditional TD of 1950, with the Y Type's independent front suspension. No less than 23,488, or close on 80 per cent of TD production, which lasted until 1953, was exported to America so paving the way for the TF, MGA and, finally, the MGB. It will be recalled that responsibility for MG car design had been

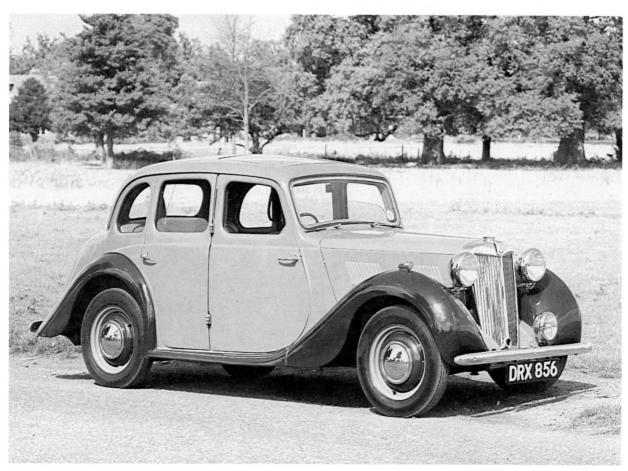

The MG Y type of 1947 shared body panels with the Series E Morris Eight though that model boasted unitary construction whilst the Abingdon product still featured a separate underslung chassis. The Y was the first MG to be fitted with independent front suspension. The coil and wishbone system designed pre-war by Alec Issigonis of Morris Minor and Mini fame, was subsequently fitted, in essence, to the TD, TF, MGA and, finally, the MGB.

vested with Cowley from 1935 but the TD was largely, and unofficially, designed at Abingdon.

The Morris group of companies, of which MG was a part, had become the Nuffield Organisation during the war, and was soon undergoing one of its periodic rationalisations. Harold Ryder was sacked in December 1947 and S.V. Smith took over responsibility for MG. Wolseley production was transferred to Cowley while Riley car assembly was moved to the MG factory at Abingdon. Along with Riley, in 1949, came Jack Tatlow, who took over as MG's general manager, while John Thornley, who had worked at MG since 1931, became his assistant.

John William Yates Thornley (born 1909) began his career, not in the motor industry, but in the august surroundings of the offices of Peat, Marwick and Mitchell, the prestigious City of London accountants. He joined them straight from school after education at Ardingly College. 'That was my father's wish but, on my 21st birthday, a small sum of money dropped into my lap'. Up until then young Thornley had ridden motor cycles, which worried his family somewhat, so they said 'get off two wheels on to four'. Consequently, in June 1930, he went off to his local car dealer to see what was on offer. 'They had a supercharged Triumph, a Morgan and M Type MG. Of course, I chose the MG!' Then, that October, while reading *The Light Car*, he spotted a letter from one Roy Marsh of Highbury, London N.5 headed 'Why not an MG Car Club?'. So John made his way to Marsh's house, along with three others, and emerged as the first secretary of the MG Car Club. The next stage was to get the blessing of the MG company so, on the following Saturday, Thornley went to Cecil Kimber at Abingdon as he wanted his permission to use the MG name in the club's title, along with its famous octagon, in the club badge. Kimber was delighted with the idea and even commissioned F. Gordon Crosby, *The Autocar's* famous artist, to design it. Fortunately the club prospered and continues to do so until this day.

In the meantime, John, as an articled clerk, was attending evening classes for his Bachelor of Commerce degree though, simultaneously, MG Car Club membership rose to the 200 mark. Clearly, something had to go and he was determined that it was not going to be his MG involvement! Initially

John Thornley, MG's general manager from 1952 until 1969, pictured with a pre-war NE Magnette, in the export compound at Abingdon in the mid-1960s. After spending three years with city accountants Peat Marwick and Mitchell, in 1931 Thornley 'ran away to Abingdon' and became service manager in 1933. He managed the famous 'Three Musketeers' and 'Cream Crackers' trials teams in 1936 and 1938 and, after war service in the Royal Army Ordnance Corps, returned to MG. In 1947 he became sales and service manager, then assistant general manager in 1948, general manager in 1952 and a director in 1956. It was Thornley who visualised the MGB as a far better equipped and refined successor to the MGA sports car which was to prove a highly successful formula and, instead of running for its original five or so years, the B endured until 1980. In 1964 John Thornley was awarded the OBE for services to the Air Training Corps. (Courtesy John Thornley)

MGB
The illustrated history

Kimber turned a deaf ear but, eventually agreed to young Thornley's suggestion that he gave him a job and run the MG Car Club from Abingdon.

Therefore, on 3 November 1931, John Thornley reported for duty. 'I signed on and then told my father!' In addition to his club duties, he assisted the service manager and, in 1933, took over the running of that department, a position he held until the outbreak of the Second World War.

John Thornley served in the Royal Army Ordnance Corps during hostilities, when he attained the rank of lieutenant colonel, and returned to Abingdon in 1945. In 1947, Thornley became sales *and* service manager. As already noted, in 1949 the Nuffield Organisation decided to move Riley car production south to Abingdon but the original idea was to uproot MG and transfer it to Coventry, until Thornley weighed in 'with a tremendous eruption over at Cowley and got them to reverse their plans'. He much enjoyed his spell as assistant general manager and 'learnt a tremendous amount' during his three years in the job.

Corporate affairs were once again destined to overtake MG for, in 1952, came the formation of the British Motor Corporation, created by a merger of the Austin and Morris companies, and headed by Leonard Lord. He had slammed out of Cowley in 1936 after clashing with Lord Nuffield over his share of Morris Motors' growing profits. He departed, subsequently threatening to 'tear Cowley apart, brick by bloody brick' and, in 1938, had joined the rival Austin company as Lord Austin's heir apparent. Following its founder's death, by 1945 he was running the company. Lord subsequently initiated a series of overtures to Lord Nuffield that culminated in BMC's 1952 creation. Although officially described as a merger, what should have been a fusion was, in effect, a takeover of Morris by Austin, with control of corporate affairs firmly centred at Austin's headquarters at Longbridge, Birmingham. Leonard Lord was an outstanding production engineer, but could also be a vindictive individual, and once in control of BMC took the opportunity, on occasions, to chasten and humiliate certain people within the Nuffield Organisation who had opposed the creation of BMC.

Lord was keen that there should be a corporate sports car to benefit from the growing market for British sports car in America but, instead of allowing Abingdon to modernise its products and build on its growing popularity there, Lord took the

MGA genesis: EX 172, a special-bodied TD, created by Syd Enever in 1951 for *Autosport* photographer George Phillips to run in the Le Mans 24 hour race. The car's body lines were inspired by the Jaguar XK 120 and only one door was fitted, on the driver's side. He sat rather high, on account of the car's TD chassis and a 20 inch high windscreen would have been required for him to have received proper protection! Phillips had competed in the 1949 race in his special-bodied TC, when he was disqualified due to a mistake by his co-driver but, in the same car, he achieved eighteenth position and second in class in 1950. He retired after 60 laps, with a dropped valve, in this car in the 1951 race.

extraordinary decision to create *another* sports cars line. Quite unknown to MG, he commissioned prototypes from Frazer Nash, Jensen and Healey and, much to the surprise of a delighted Donald Healey, the *Austin Healey* was announced at the 1952 Motor Show. The Healey 100 was a stylish, modern 100 mph car with low, full-width bodywork and used the engine and gearbox from the redundant Austin Atlantic saloon. When production began in 1953, it was soon out-selling the archaic MG TD, with its roots firmly planted in the 1930s.

The paradox was that MG had spontaneously and clandestinely seized the initiative and developed its own modern prototype in 1952. The car was completed late in the year and represented the first link in a chain of events which culminated in the arrival of the MGA in 1955 and its MGB derivative seven years later. These three projects were all conceived by Albert Sydney Enever, MG's chief engineer, who had joined the company in 1928.

Syd Enever is one of a family of eight children and was born at Colden Common, near Winchester in Hampshire in 1906. His father, Francis Albert, was an ironmonger's

assistant though he later served an apprenticeship making stained glass windows. Maud Matilda, his mother, hailed from Littlemore, near Oxford where her parents were dairy farmers who had a butchers shop, bakehouse and dairy on the Cowley to Oxford Road. Unfortunately Syd's parents separated when he was three and his mother subsequently took her large family to a more familiar Oxford, where she opened a theatrical boarding house. Like many youngsters, Enever's interest in wheeled vehicles surfaced early on. He designed, and made, a crude cart from wood and pram wheels, but was disappointed when a winged version failed to take off .... Becoming more ambitious, he built a boat but was alarmed to find that, being too wide and stubby, it would not steer properly and only 'went around in circles'.

Syd's strong practical ability, complemented by a precocious interest in mechanical matters, came to the attention of Mr Benson, the headmaster of his South Oxford School. It is to his eternal credit that, in 1921, he got 15-year-old Sydney Enever a job in the Morris Garages sales rooms in Queens Street, Oxford. His wage was 12s 6d a week and young Syd began work as an errand boy, riding a bicycle with the garage's name displayed on a sign attached to the crossbar. After about a year, Syd was transferred to one of the firm's garages behind the Clarendon Hotel. There he developed a reputation for quick, intuitive responses to mechanical maladies and, on one celebrated occasion, one Sunday changed the big ends on a Morris Cowley in an astounding 20 minutes. This achievement soon entered Morris Gar-

ages lore because the time-related charge of £4.10s raised eyebrows, to say the least, in the accounts department.

It was as a 20-year-old in 1926 that young Enever bought a 3.5 hp BSA motor cycle. He experimented with tuning the unit, and raised the compression ratio by bolting a thin steel plate to the top of the piston, which worked well enough until the overstressed component melted. He also built his first crude car at about the same time. It was a three-wheeler, powered by an old BSA engine, which may have been the one from the luckless motorcycle!

The following year came the move to Abingdon. Syd Enever was no stranger to the former leather works, as he had prepared used cars for sale there, when it served as a vehicle store. It says much for his abilities that he was assigned to the firm's experimental department headed by Cecil (Cec) Cousins. Enever subsequently became department head and, when responsibility for the design of MG cars was transferred to Cowley, he remained behind at Abingdon in a liaison role. He was involved in some fascinating projects. There were thoughts about a V8-engined saloon with all independent suspension on the lines of the R type racing car, but this came to nothing. By contrast, the record breaking EX 135 was built. This began life as the celebrated Magic Magnette of 1934. Enever worked on its supercharged 1100 cc six-cylinder engine with Reg Jackson, another MG stalwart, while Reid Railton, who was also responsible for John Cobb's Land Speed Record Napier Railton, designed the new, streamlined bodywork. Driven by

Major
Goldie Gardner,   it ran on German autobhans in 1938 and 1939, and, on the latter occasion, achieved 203.5 mph for the Flying Kilometer and 203.2 mph for the Flying Mile, a record that stands to this day. Afterwards, and only three months before the outbreak of the Second World War, Gardner, accompanied by Syd Enever and Reg Jackson, made a clandestine visit to the Horch factory at Zwickau, Saxony, where the mid-engined Auto Union racing cars were built, the trip having been arranged by the cars' celebrated designer, Robert Eberan von Eberhorst.

Syd had been promoted to be MG's chief planning engineer in 1938 and, during the war, he was involved in Sherman and Centaur tank conversion work then being undertaken at Abingdon. With the coming of peace, in 1946 Syd Enever again attended EX 135's record breaking activities, but also became more directly concerned with the design of road cars. His first post-war project was the TD, which he speedily created with Cec Cousins in the face of falling TC sales. Then, in 1951, came a special TD for *Autosport* photographer George Phillips to run at that year's Le Mans race. Quietly prepared by Syd at Abingdon, with bodywork clearly inspired by the Jaguar XK 120, this car really marks the starting point of the MGA, for Enever took its lines for the previously mentioned 1952 MG prototype. He later recalled that he 'designed every nut, bolt and screw of it . . .' It was a car which started out in life on the dining

Syd Enever took the concept of the Phillips car one stage further in 1952 when he produced EX 175, which was effectively the prototype MGA and employed a new box-section chassis. It was virtually identical to the finished product with the obvious exception of the high TD engine, which demanded the bonnet bulge, while there were minor differences to the windscreen, bumpers and front valance. Alas, BMC's Leonard Lord rejected this burgundy prototype in favour of the Healey 100 and it was to be another three years before the MGA entered production.

room table of his Oxford home at 76, Southern Bypass, Botley; this car was coded EX 175. I should explain that the EX (for experiment) numbers which will continue to pepper this text relate to projects that originated from MG's drawing office. Those cars that were funded on a BMC budget, or were Longbridge inspired, carried the ADO prefix, though whether this stood for Austin, or Amalgamated – following the BMC merger – Drawing Office, is unclear. Once an MG design received corporate approval, however, it was invariably allotted an ADO number in addition to its EX one. But to return to EX 175. The visual resemblance to the 1951 Phillips' TD ended there, for it was a very different car beneath the bodywork. One of its shortcomings had been its TD chassis, which meant that the driver sat rather high, *on* rather than *in* the car. EX 175 therefore had a new, wider box section chassis, (a spare was made at the same time) which resulted in an improved seating position, with the driver sitting much lower in the car.

If 1952 was a disappointing year for Abingdon, with BMC's refusal to sanction EX 175's production, in another sense it was one of great significance for MG. The creation of BMC resulted in the departure of Jack Tatlow, its general manager, for Morris Commercial in Birmingham. In November of the year, his place was taken by John Thornley, twenty-one years to the day after he had joined the company. It was a crucial appointment, when viewed in the light of

Syd Enever, MG's chief engineer from 1954 until 1971. This outstanding and intuitive engineer was responsible for engineering, amongst other projects, the EX 179 and EX 181 record cars and the MGA and MGB. He joined Morris Garages in 1921 and the MG Car Company in 1928. Following the move to Abingdon, he subsequently rose to head the firm's experimental department until 1938 when he became chief planning engineer. He continued in that capacity after the war, a position he held until 1954, when he was promoted to chief engineer. (Courtesy Syd Enever)

future events, for it meant that MG was headed by an enthusiastic, articulate manager to champion the MG cause within the BMC orbit. When talking to John Thornley the reason why Abingdon was such a happy and successful place in its heyday becomes readily apparent. A bubbling sense of humour is never far below the surface and he readily admits that he had made it part of his philosophy of life to use 'laughter as the lubricant' particularly when the going is tough.

Although Abingdon was stuck with the TD, 1953 saw the arrival of a 'new' MG saloon, to replace the Y type, which had also been styled pre-war and was showing its years. Design was still officially vested in Cowley, where a specific department was responsible for MG, Riley and Wolseley projects and operated under Gerald Palmer's direction. Palmer, who had been involved in the Y's creation, had left Cowley in 1942 and journeyed north to the Jowett company of Idle, Yorkshire where he designed its advanced Javelin saloon. He returned to the Nuffield fold in 1949, and was responsible for the overall conception of the Wolseley 4/44 saloon of 1952, which used the Y type's XPAG engine. But the creation of BMC in the same year resulted in a stringent engine rationalisation programme and when the MG equivalent of the Wolseley, the Z Series Magnette, (which revived a famous pre-war MG name) arrived in 1953 it was the first Abingdon product to be powered by the BMC B Series engine, which was an Austin design.

This power unit was of great significance to MG, as it was to power also the MGA and, subsequently, the MGB, so its origins are of relevance to our story. Pre-war, all Austin car engines had been side valvers and the first of a new generation of overhead valve ones was the 2.2 litre unit used in the Austin 16 of 1945 and later, incidentally, in the Austin Healey 100. That engine had been developed during the war and was a four-cylinder version of a six-cylinder truck engine introduced at Longbridge in 1938. At the end of the war, work began on a new, small capacity unit, with intended capacities of 900cc and 1200cc, though eventually only the larger size reached production. It followed the general lines of the 16 hp unit, having a sturdy three-bearing crankshaft, while the pushrods, manifolds and carburettor were on the

MG's first monocoque was the Z type Magnette saloon of 1954. Sharing many body components with the Wolseley 4/44 of 1953, it was the first Austin/engined MG, its 1489cc four having been redesignated the BMC B Series unit following the creation of the British Motor Corporation in 1952. The engine was also shared with the MGA sports car of 1955 and was finally fitted, in enlarged 1798cc form, in the MGB.

left-hand side, well away from the distributor, dynamo and starter motor on the right. The new engine first appeared in the Austin A40 Devon and Dorset saloons in 1948. Following the creation of BMC, the engine was designated the B Series unit, the smaller 803cc one, which powered the Austin A30 of 1951, being the A Series. (The C Series, a 2.6 litre six, did not arrive until 1954 and, unlike the A and B engines, which were conceived at Longbridge, the big six was designed by Morris Engines at Coventry).

The arrival of the Magnette, which was

also the first MG with unitary construction bodywork, saw the B Series engine revamped, with the capacity upped to 1489cc, achieved by increasing the size of the 65mm bore to 73mm. Twin carburettors, in keeping with MG's sporting traditions, were fitted; 12,754 saloons were built between 1953 and 1955.

By 1953, with the EX175 project sidelined, the situation on the MG sports car front was looking predictably bleak. TD output had dropped from a near 11,000 peak in 1952 to 6510 in 1953. That year, however, saw the arrival of the last of the T Series Midgets: the TF. This was a mildly reworked TD, with a handsome, sloping radiator, integral headlamps, and a stylish rear. But, of all the T type sports cars, it was destined to sell the least, 9600 having been built by the time that production ceased in 1955.

The engine used in the TF in its original form was the 1250cc EXPAG unit and virtually the same as that used in the TD. In the second half of 1953, however, George Eyston, whose MG record breaking activities had begun in 1930, made a direct approach to Leonard Lord and suggested that MG produce a new, special car for him. Eyston, who had spent much of his life in America, wanted to take up Gardner's record breaking baton, and also give MG's trans-Atlantic sales a much needed boost. Lord, who held Eyston in high regard, agreed. In the first instance, the EX 175 prototype of 1952 was fitted with wheel spats, an undershield and a perspex cockpit and was then submitted to wind tunnel testing. The results, though, were disappointing and, additionally, there were strong marketing objections to fielding publicly what was a prototype car. So Syd Enever took the spare chassis he had prudently had constructed when EX 175 was built, and this formed the basis of EX 179, a new MG record car for which he designed a streamlined body, resembling that of EX 135. It was powered by a 1496cc version of the EXPAG engine, achieved by upping the bore size from 69 to 72mm, a capacity which had been unofficially attained by MG enthusiasts. BMC decided to adopt this increase in the light of improved casting techniques, in response to MG's American customers who were crying out for a more powerful version of the TF. It was decided to introduce the newly designated EXPEG unit in 1954 though a plan to announce it to coincide with the record attempt misfired because a backlog of 1250cc units had first to be seen through before the engine entered production, for export markets only, in November of 1954.

EX 179 duly secured a clutch of long distance records in August 1954, but the big event of the year had come in June when Sir Leonard Lord, as he became in the New Year Honours, gave MG permission to put EX 175 into production. 'The fact that we'd produced it showed we were capable of designing our own cars', recalls John Thornley, 'also I think that he had a bit of a conscience that he treated us a little unfairly in 1952'. This meant that the drawing office, closed in 1935, was reopened and staff recruited from Cowley. In addition, the Corporation agreed that a competition programme be restarted after a 20 year hiatus and Marcus Chambers, a one time member of the HRG racing team, was appointed to manage it. Although the emphasis was placed on rallying, corporate permission was obtained to launch the revived EX 175 design at the Le Mans 24 hour race in June

1955. To round-off the 1954 package, Syd Enever was given the title of chief engineer, a rôle he had been unofficially undertaking for years! Had Cecil Kimber lived he could only have approved of these enlightened decisions.

The new car was called the MGA, a designation suggested by Thornley who recalls Abingdon had 'run out of alphabet', having reached Z with the Magnette. The arrival of the new sports car represented a new chapter in MG's history. 'At one hit, here is a title which signifies a new beginning and which also compels the use of the MG name whenever reference is made to it', he wrote in 1956, adding, 'What is more, there can be 25 more models before the problem recurs!'

Unfortunately the MGA's launch was delayed, due to hold-ups with body tooling, but three cars, visually almost identical to the production versions, were run in the 24 hour classic in EX 182 guise. Although the 1952 EX 175 prototype had used the TD's 1250cc engine, the A used the BMC B Series unit, of similar specification to that employed in thé ZA Magnette saloon. The delays meant that MGA production had not begun until August so a mere 1003 examples were made by the end of the year. This model change meant that only 2463 MG sports cars were built in 1955, the lowest figure since 1947. However, 1956's MGA production stood at 13,410, the highest annual sports car figure then achieved by Abingdon. With a further 20,571 MGAs made in 1957, the model was well on its way to becoming the most successful MG sports car yet built.

While the MGA was entering production, the versatile Enever was, once again, turning his attention to record breaking. EX 179, like its pre-war EX 135 predecessor, had been front-engined but this location dictated the height of the car's nose. A lower profile would have resulted in a more aerodynamically efficient shape, and for this new MG record breaker, designated EX 181, he positioned the engine behind the driver in the manner of Railton's Land Speed Record car. The power unit was an experimental supercharged twin overhead camshaft engine of 1489cc, destined to appear in unblown 1588cc form in the Twin Cam MGA of 1958/60. With the engine thus relegated to a less intrusive position, Enever conceived a low, tear drop shaped body, following tests at Armstrong Whitworth's

MGB
The illustrated history

wind tunnel at Baginton, near Coventry and inspired by the cross section of the experimental AW 52 Flying Wing aircraft. Working under Enever's direction, MG's Terry Mitch-

With the MGA safely into production, Syd Enever began work on EX 181, what was to be MG's last record breaking car. These models, which John Thornley dubbed 'Enever's toys', were produced for wind tunnel feasibility studies in 1956. MG used the Armstrong Whitworth facility at Baginton, near Coventry and are: left to right, two versions of EX 135, NSU world record breaking motor cycle and two variations on the EX 181 theme. Enever was investigating the possibility of incorporating the advantages of ground effect at this time.

ell was responsible for translating these experiments on to paper. EX 181 was only 38.5 inches high to the top of the driver's cowl and 15 feet 1.5 inches long.

When it came to the ticklish matter of obtaining BMC funding for EX 181, John Thornley adopted a technique he was to apply when seeking finance for production cars. Choosing the timing of his approach with care, he presented the corporation with a *fait accompli,* by which time the project was sufficiently advanced it would have been imprudent to have cancelled it!

In August 1957, with Stirling Moss at the wheel, EX 181 established five new Class F records and attained a top speed of 245.64 mph. Later, in September 1959, with 181's engine enlarged to 1506cc to qualify for Class E regulations and with minor modifications to the bodywork, Phil Hill improved on this figure and achieved 254.91 mph over the flying kilometre. This was the last occasion on which MG went record breaking.

With EX 181 completed, John Thornley and Syd Enever began thinking in terms of a

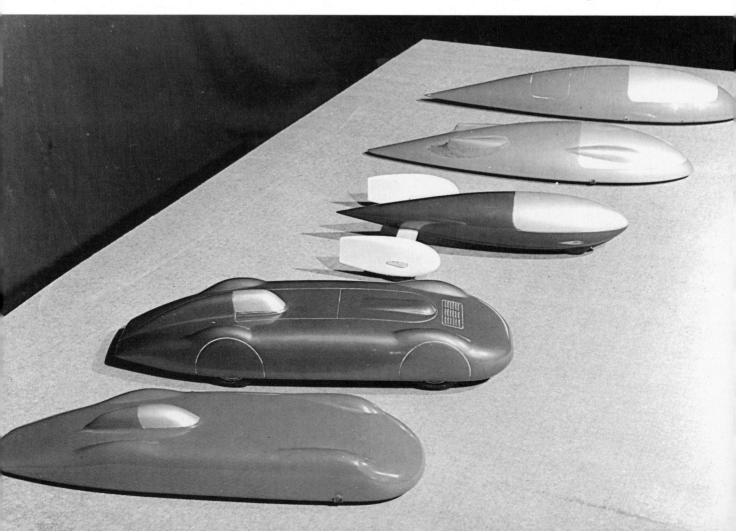

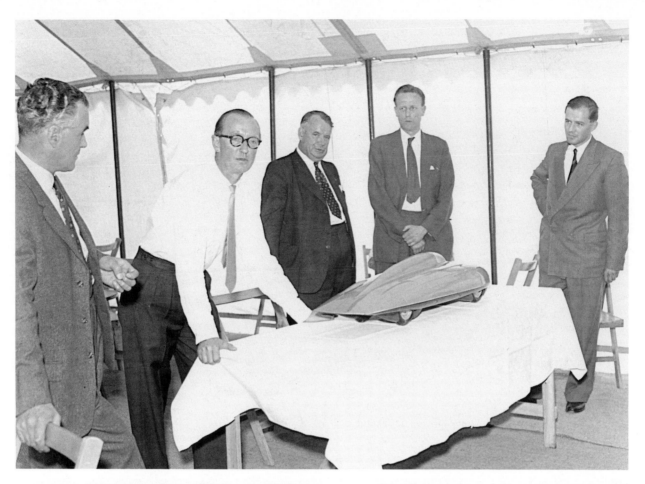

John Thornley, with the definitive quarter-scale model of EX 181, with body lines by MG's Terry Mitchell. Syd Enever is on Thornley's right and Eddie Maher, Morris Engines' chief experimental engineer, who was responsible for the development of its 1489cc twin overhead camshaft Shorrock supercharged engine, on his left. Jack Goffin, Morris Engines' assistant chief experimental engineer, is on the extreme right of the photograph.

replacement for the MGA. Thornley's thoughts had already jelled by this time. 'My imagination was fired by seeing a trio of Aston Martin DB2/4 coupés competing in a production car race at Silverstone. I can remember seeing the three of them, side by side, on the track, to this day. I thought "that's the shape our new car ought to be"'. Thus it will be seen that, at its genesis, the MGB was conceived as a *closed* rather than open car, a configuration which finally appeared as the GT in 1965. But there was never any question that the MGA's successor, in the first instance, would be anything but open.

Simultaneously ideas began to evolve regarding the new model's appearance and the new EX 205 number for it was issued in 1957 for what the company's design register simply describes as 'MG 2-seater (MGB)'. So Syd Enever got MG's chief body engineer, Jim O'Neill, to design a coupé clearly derived from the EX 181 record breaker. EX 205/1 was, by all accounts, 'a very fat, sexy looking lady' and with such parentage, she had curvy, aerodynamically acceptable styling. There were good commercial arguments for producing a road car so obviously derived from a record breaker but, as is so often the way with a vehicle possessing a low drag coefficient, it lacked visual appeal. EX 205/1, which was made in model form only, was no exception.

When it came to ideas about an open car, there was a styling exercise by Frua, the Turin-based stylist, which was given a free hand to produce a two-seater roadster body on an MGA 1500 chassis. Its creation came at a time when British motor manufacturers were waking up to the fact that one-off cars and prototypes could be quickly, and often cheaply, produced by Italian styling and coachbuilding establishments. When the car was returned to Abingdon in 1957, finished

Early thoughts about the MGA's replacement resulted in this Frua-styled roadster on a 1500 A chassis in 1957. It not only looked heavy, it was, and convinced Syd Enever that the new car would have to be of monocoque construction. It was broken up soon afterwards as no import duty had been paid, though drawings made from it, designated EX 205/2R, were produced.

in vivid Ferrari red, it did not meet with general approval, which is perhaps a polite way of putting it! Not only was it a weighty car, with poor performance – which was in any case incidental because it was a styling exercise – it also *looked* heavy. Drawings were taken from the body and these, designated EX 205/2R, were completed on 20 June 1957. But the car's days were numbered because it had come to Abingdon on an import bond which meant that no duty had been paid on it. Unless one was forthcoming, it had to be exported or destroyed, and the latter was duly carried out under the watchful eye of Mr Fishpool, the local customs and excise inspector, who was based at nearby Abingdon airport. One item

The same car, photographed from the rear with the hood up with MG badge above the number plate mounting and distinctive silencer, even though the car was a poor performer!

to be spared the welder's torch was the stylish hardtop that came with the car, which somehow got overlooked. It was this car that convinced Syd Enever that he would dispense with any idea of retaining the MGA's chassis for its successor and opt for smaller, neater monocoque body construction.

There were a number of reasons for this decision being taken. One was simply geographical. The Cowley-based Pressed Steel Company was in the process of building a new factory at nearby Swindon, on which more anon, which was geared for unitary body construction. Also the process was gradually extending from high production saloons to the lower output sports car sector. BMC's first was the Austin Healey Sprite of 1958. Rootes' Sunbeam Alpine two-seater, announced in mid-1959, also used this construction and Jaguar's first sports car monocoque, the D-type derived E-type, was just a

further two years away. To the engineer, a monocoque offered a rigid, light body structure but these advantages were offset by initial high tooling costs which demanded a high quantity production run to recoup outlay. This would come, not from the home market, but from the vast potential of American sales. MGs trans-Atlantic appeal reached back to the post war TC and with the success of the TD and MGA it was felt by Abingdon that the MGB replacement would overhaul the A's record sales. In addition to this, the A's chassis was assembled by MG, just the side members being obtained from John Thompson Pressings of Wolverhampton, and welding up the frame was a labour intensive exercise that took up valuable space in the Abingdon press shop. A monocoque MG would completely eliminate that stage of the manufacturing process.

It was also decided to broaden the new model's appeal, perhaps the most subtle part of the MGB design exercise. The MGA had, in concept, been an out-and-out sports car with suspension to match. In open form it retained separate side screens and the dashboard didn't even contain a glove compartment. For its successor, Thornley and Enever decided to soften up the suspension, introduce wind-up windows, offer a roomier cockpit and include such niceties as a glove compartment, while not diluting the car's undoubted sporting pedigree. The MGB, as it eventually appeared in 1962 was, in truth, closer to a high-speed tourer than a sports car but the success of the package is borne out by the fact that the B overhauled the A's 100,000 odd units within four years of its arrival.

The crucial suspension improvements were undertaken by Enever and his chief draughtsman, Roy Brocklehurst. Before considering the work that was undertaken, it is first necessary to consider Brocklehurst's career with MG for his layout of the MGB's mechanical components, meant that he played a formative role in the model's conception. Roy Brocklehurst (born 1932) joined the MG Car Company straight from school in June 1947, as a design apprentice. 'I wanted to get into engineering badly, not necessarily cars but engineering'. Roy grew up at nearby Didcot so, in mid-1947, he cycled over to the recently opened Atomic Energy Research Establishment at Harwell to enquire whether there were any apprenticeships available. As it happened, there

'Well it's only flat at the bottom!' This light-hearted photograph first appeared in MG's *Safety Fast* magazine. The car is a prototype MG Midget – it was nearly the MGD – the MG version of the Austin Healey Sprite, introduced in 1961. Its luckless 'owner' surveying his workshop manual, is Roy Brocklehurst who joined MG as a design apprentice in 1947, became chief draughtsman in 1956 and assistant chief engineer in 1964. He was responsible for detailing the MGB's mechanical layout and,

in 1971, succeeded Syd Enever as MG's chief engineer. In 1973, he left Abingdon and moved to Longbridge, having been made Austin Morris's chief engineer, vehicle engineering, and subsequently became closely involved with the design and development of the all-important Austin Metro. In 1980 Brocklehurst was appointed chief engineer advanced vehicles at BL Technology's Gaydon facility. He retired in 1987. (Courtesy Roy Brocklehurst)

weren't at the time, so he kept on pedalling until he arrived at the MG factory at Abingdon, complete with a bundle of drawings! There he saw personnel officer Joan Brewer and later Syd Enever. As a result he got the job as a design apprentice and, by December 1948 at the grand old age of $16^{1}/_{2}$, he was drawing the special three-throw crankshaft for Goldie Gardner's EX 135 which was to run on three of its six cylinders for a successful 1949 500cc record attempt.

At this time MG was building TCs at Abingdon but, as we've seen, the TD was unofficially designed there. Roy was responsible for the independent front suspension layout for the TD and its TF successor 'as they were only conversions from the Y type saloon'. As the new models were supposed to emanate from Cowley Roy recalls that he was the only design draughtsman at Abingdon at the time! He used to attend the Oxford College of Technology for his theoretical training. 'I'd cadge a lift into Oxford on the T Series cars being driven to Nuffield Exports at Cowley for overseas markets'. In 1952 Brocklehurst left Abingdon for two years National Service in the RAF but not before he had completed the chassis drawings for EX 175 which was, as we have seen, the prototype MGA.

On his return to the factory, in June 1954, he was promoted to the post of layout draughtsman and was pleased to find that he had some new colleagues, that being the pivotal year when the MG design office was re-opened. 'Syd Enever had ''imported'' four draughtsmen from Cowley, two on chassis work and two on bodies,' Roy remembers. Efforts were concentrated on getting the MGA into production and this was a particularly interesting time for Brocklehurst as it was the first complete vehicle he'd ever been concerned with; hitherto his involvement had been with individual components and one-off projects.

The MGA finally reached the public in the autumn of 1955 and soon afterwards, as we've seen, the profile of its successor began to emerge and Roy's particular involvement was with the rear suspension of the new MGB. 'We were looking for lower suspension rates and greater wheel travel. If you stay with half elliptic springs then they have to get longer. Then you get into tramp problems. A coil spring/radius arm configuration has *got* to be better'. So it was decided to adopt the latter layout for the

MGA's successor and tests were carried out on simulators (modified MGAs). It was while testing one of these cars, also fitted with a transverse Watts linkage, that Roy and his passenger were involved in a dramatic accident, fortunately without injury to themselves, when a rear wheel got trapped inside its arch on a corner at nearby Boars Hill, the MGA cartwheeling tail over nose before coming to rest. After a concentrated series of experiments, Enever and Brocklehurst finally arrived at a rear suspension layout with trailing radius arms, coil springs and with the live rear axle laterally located by a Panhard rod. Even though the Watts linkage had the advantage of common characteristics on cornering, it was dispensed with on cost grounds.

Meanwhile, by 1958, the first full scale monocoque body was taking shape in wooden mock-up form at Morris Bodies factory at Quinton Road, Coventry. It was a coupé designed by Donald (Don) Hayter (born 1927) and, as he later went on to style the MGB proper his career, prior to joining MG early in 1956, is of considerable relevance to our story. Don Hayter went to the Pressed Steel Company at Cowley straight from school in 1942. At the time the firm was producing complete fuselages and tail sections for such famous wartime aircraft as the Spitfire, Wellington and Lancaster. Don's role was to translate the plans supplied by the plane's manufacturers into production drawings.

The end of the war in 1945 saw Pressed Steel's car body jigs removed from storage and renovated so, inevitably, the first British cars of the post war years were 'thirties carry-overs'. The first really exciting car with which Hayter was involved was the XK 120 which Jaguar had initially produced in aluminium bodied form. His job was to interpret existing schemes and streamline them so the panels would come off the tools properly. He recalls conducting a similar exercise with the MG ZA Magnette which went into production at Abingdon in 1953. Don remained at Pressed Steel until early 1954 when 'I realised that I was learning more and more about less and less in that I was an expert on steel bodywork. But I wasn't seeing the whole car because I wasn't in at the start'. He therefore decided to leave Cowley and join a car manufacturer so he could become involved with the styling of the vehicle itself.

As luck would have it, Don saw an advertisement in *The Autocar* for a draughtsman with Aston Martin, at that time based at Feltham, Middlesex. He applied and got the job and found he was working under Frank Feeley's direction. Feeley had styled the V12 Lagonda before the war and had been responsible for the coachwork of all the post-war Aston Martins prior to the DB4 of 1958. One of Don Hayter's first styling assignments was a new radiator shape for the Aston Martin DB3 which appeared in 1957. David Brown, who owned the firm was a frequent visitor. 'You'd do a sketch and he'd say "I like that, turn it into a quarter scale model" and Ernie Game, the model maker there, would produce one.'

By this time the range of Aston Martin passenger cars was due to be replaced by a new four-seater GT, the DB4. This was to be a completely new car and manager John Wyer's decision to go to Touring of Milan for its body styling was a particularly inspired one. Don Hayter drew the lines for the sort of shape Aston Martin had in mind 'and these were sent to Touring who did a longer version of the prototype already built at Feltham'. He was much enjoying his time at Aston Martin but, in 1955, David Brown purchased the Newport Pagnell based Tickford company and staff began moving up there. Don didn't want to go 'so I wondered about MG and wrote to them on spec. Funnily enough they'd been advertising recently and hadn't received any replies. So I went to see Syd Enever and got the job of chief body draughtsman'. Bearing in mind John Thornley's admiration for the Aston Martin DB 2/4 theme, Don Hayter's

Overleaf: **The MGA, introduced in 1955, was MG's most successful sports car prior to the introduction of the MGB. By the time that production ceased in 1962, a total of 101,081 (98,970 pushrod and 2111 twin-cam cars) had been built. In essence, the A's engine, gearbox, rear axle, suspension, steering, petrol tank and twin six volt battery layout were carried over to the MGB. However, the most significant difference between the two cars was that the MGA boasted a substantial box section chassis. The A turned the scales in open form at 17.75 cwt while the MGB, although a monocoque, was heavier, at 18.5 cwt. (Courtesy Quadrant/Autocar)**

31

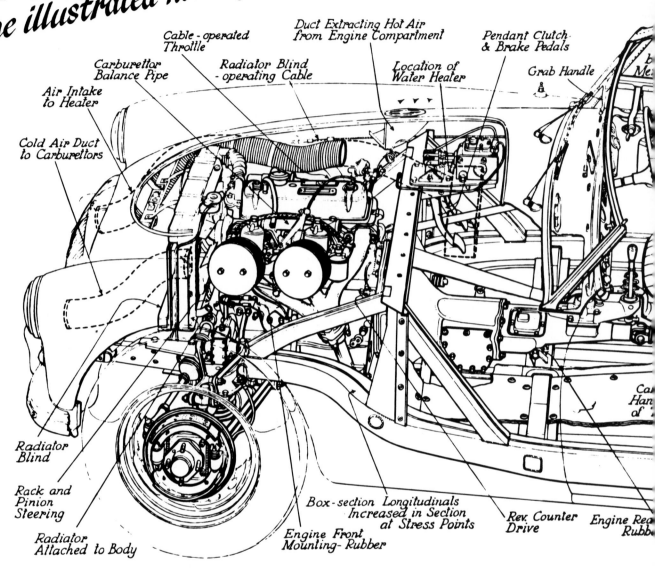

Air Intake
to Heater

Carburettor
Balance Pipe

Cable - operated
Throttle

Radiator Blind
- operating Cable

Duct Extracting Hot Air
from Engine Compartment

Location of
Water Heater

Pendant Clutch
& Brake Pedals

Grab Handle

Cold Air Duct
to Carburettors

Radiator
Blind

Rack and
Pinion
Steering

Radiator
Attached to Body

Engine Front
Mounting- Rubber

Box - section Longitudinals
Increased in Section
at Stress Points

Rev. Counter
Drive

Engine Rea
Rubb

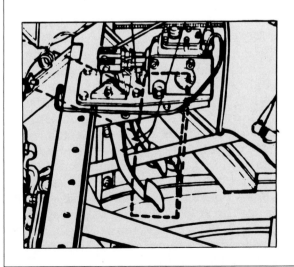

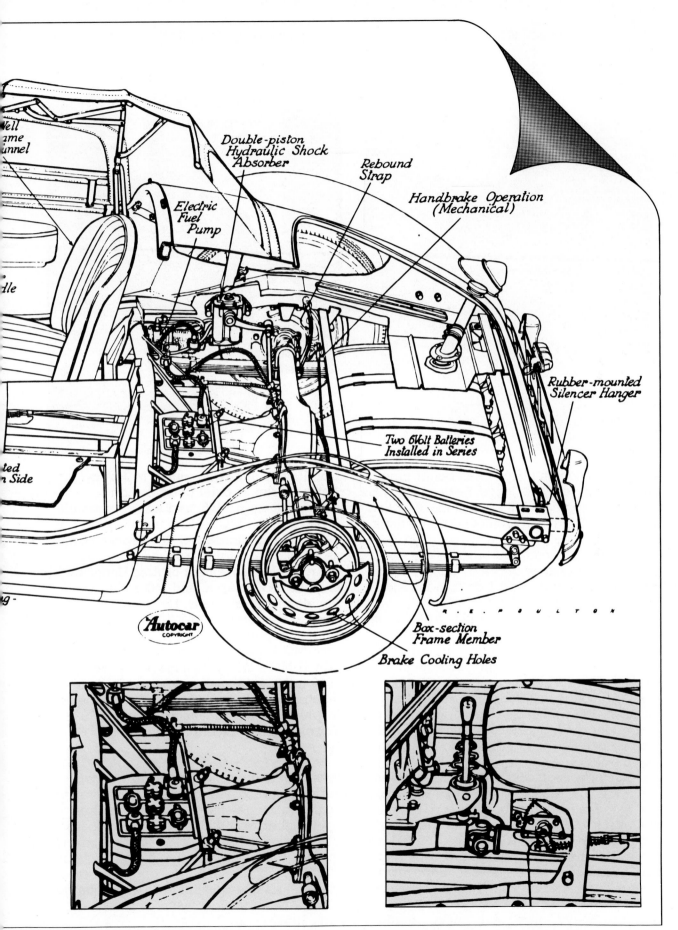

Well
...ame
...unnel

Double-piston
Hydraulic Shock
Absorber

Rebound
Strap

Handbrake Operation
(Mechanical)

Electric
Fuel
Pump

...dle

Rubber-mounted
Silencer Hanger

Two 6Volt Batteries
Installed in Series

...ted
...n Side

Autocar
COPYRIGHT

R. E. POULTON

Box-section
Frame Member

Brake Cooling Holes

...g -

33

application couldn't have been better timed, but he was sorry to leave Feltham. 'I was there for two years but I learnt more in that time by working long hours than you'd think. Also Frank Feeley was a great guy. He'd give you your head and say "let's make a model and see how it comes out". All this experience would stand Don in good stead when he moved to MG.

When he went to Abingdon, in February 1956, the first job he did was to design the detachable panels in the wheel arches of the Twin Cam MGA to permit access to the exhaust pipes. Then there was the styling of the MGA coupé that Ted Lund first ran at Le Mans in 1960. The car had originally appeared there in roadster form and they said, 'you've been at Aston Martin, do something like the DB3S coupé'.

Hayter's next coupé design, as we've seen, was in the EX 205 series and was a full size wooden mock-up, built at Morris Bodies at Coventry, which echoed John Thornley's 'poor man's Aston Martin' theme. 'I lived up there for a time doing the job and John and Syd used to come up to see how it was going'. But Hayter reckoned that the finished product reminded him of a war horse in full armour 'heavy, nice and curvy, getting

Don Hayter, left, who joined MG from Aston Martin as chief body design draughtsman in 1955, and was responsible for styling the MGB. He is pictured here, in 1974, having succeeded Roy Brocklehurst as MG's chief engineer in the previous year, on the retirement of Alec Hounslow, another MG veteran, and MG's chief development engineer. He is receiving a copy of *The Story of the MG Sports Car,* originally published in 1972, the work of arch-MG historian Wilson McComb, who edited MG's *Safety Fast* magazine from 1959 to 1964. Hounslow served as a riding mechanic in Tazio Nuvolari's K3 Magnette, in which the Italian maestro won the 1933 Tourist Trophy race. (Courtesy Don Hayter)

there but still wrong'. That was the concensus so Don returned to Abingdon and started again from scratch but this time he drew an open rather than a closed car. 'I took a new EX number, 214, and 214/1 was drawn quarter-scale straight on to the paper which I then gave to Harry Herring, our model maker, and that was the MGB all in one go'. This pencil drawing was completed on 19 June 1958.

A quarter-scale model of 1958 of a possible MGA replacement (on an MGA chassis) of the Frua-styled roadster. The distinctive radiator grille treatment, sidelights and stepped rear wings are all to be found on the one car bodied by the Italian company.

MG's chief body engineer, Jim O'Neill, was responsible for the lines of this GT version of the Frua design, which has strong similarities to the contemporary Aston Martin DB4 of 1958.

This roadster in the EX 205 series, the work of Don Hayter, was completed in 1958. Still utilising the MGA chassis, it is moving towards the definitive MGB lines, with the headlamps and the side and flasher units already bearing a similarity to the finished product. However, the frontal treatment, with the MGA-derived radiator grille, which was similar to that employed on the full-sized GT mock-up produced in the same year, has yet to be resolved.

Rear view of the same model. The similarity to the production MGB is all too obvious with the rear wings, bumpers, boot lid and even the hood being subsequently transferred to Hayter's EX 214/1: the MGB.

MG variants: Superlative scale models of the possible MGA replacements, designed in 1957 and the work of MG's model maker, Harry Herring. Left to right: GT version of the Frua roadster with Ferrari influence apparent; EX 205/1, with MGA chassis, and lines inspired by EX 181 record car, with Frua-like radiator grille, the work of MG's chief body engineer, Jim O'Neill; and Don Hayter's design in this EX 205 series, with MGA-like radiator grille.

The Mark 1 Aston Martin DB2/4 of 1953, the model which inspired John Thornley's thoughts for the MGA replacement, was styled by Frank Feeley, for whom Don Hayter worked. Don was responsible for detailing the Mark 11 and Mark 111 visual facelifts during his time at Feltham.

So what were the influences that dictated the shape of the MGB roadster? Don's starting point was the EX 181 record car, and the bonnet line and side profiles were derived from that source. The front of the car, with the headlamps set back in sculptured recesses, are clearly Ferrari inspired and Hayter recalls being particularly impressed by a 2 litre example driven by Reg Parnell in 1955. EX 205/1 had a long front end but Don decided to chop it off at right angles and this gave him the shape of the radiator intake. The small embryo tail

One of Don Hayter's early assignments was to produce this MGA coupé, which had previously run in open form at Le Mans in 1959. It appeared in this closed form, finished in the same light green paint as the EX 181 record breaker, for the first time in 1960, with its twin cam engine enlarged to 1762cc. Driven by Ted Lund and Colin Escot, it finished twelfth and won the 2 litre class. It ran in 1961 but retired with engine failure.

MGB
The illustrated history

fins were a concession to current fashion though the public, unknowingly, got a preview of the B's rear end well over a year before they appeared on the new model. 'Dennis Williams, who was doing the rear end of the MG Midget at Abingdon at the

Unlike the EX 135 and EX 179 record breakers, which had front-mounted engines, that of EX 181, or Roaring Raindrop as it was known, was located behind the driver. It initially ran at the Utah salts flats, USA in August 1957, where it took five Class F records in 1489cc form. It returned in October 1959, though this time without a rear stabilising fin, and driven by Phil Hill, when enlarged to 1506cc, it took six Class E records and achieved a speed of 254.9 mph making it the fastest MG ever. It took Hill three miles to stop after this attempt because of its single disc brake, mounted on the offside of the differential. The hills in the background are, incidentally, 15 miles away! After this success, the car returned to Britain and, although later damaged in a test run, was subsequently rebuilt by MG apprentices and today forms part of the Heritage Collection.

time, copied the B's back half but that went into production sooner because it was purely a reskinned Austin Healey Sprite whereas the MGB was a brand new car and took longer to complete'. There were also some thoughts at one time of giving the B rather more pronounced rear fins in the manner of the contemporary Sunbeam Rapier but Don realised that there would be production problems, for it should be remembered that the entire MGB project was a very cost-conscious exercise. Fortunately he was ideally qualified for this work with his Aston Martin and Pressed Steel background. 'We were very aware that we had a low production car so it was vital to keep the body tooling as simple as possible'.

Once the EX 214/1 model was completed, John Thornley took it to the BMC headquarters at Longbridge for approval by the Corporation's hierachy. 'The message was, OK, go full size,' recalls Hayter, and the project received its corporate ADO 23 project number. This full size mock-up was again executed by Morris Bodies at Coventry but first the full size drawings had to be done. These were completed at Abingdon on two 18 foot long tables, one showing the body and the other the car's mechanical components. Two sets were printed off, one going to Coventry and the other to Pressed Steel, which was going to build the new car's body.

On a wooden mock-up the various component parts of the car come together like a big jig saw and they are then realistically painted. This had the advantage that after a particular model was given the go ahead, the sections were then used as masters for the first hand-made set of body

The first full-size version of the MGA's replacement was styled by Don Hayter – the Aston Martin influence is apparent – and built by Morris Bodies at Quinton Road, Coventry in 1958. His starting point was 205/1, note the rear wing profile and paint treatment, while the radiator grille echoes that of the MGA one on the model of the roadster in the earlier photograph. Hayter likens it to a war horse in full armour: 'heavy, nice and curvy, getting there but still wrong!' The design was allocated a coding in the EX 205 series.

panels. With the mock-up completed, the BMC higher echelons gave their approval. Fortunately there were virtually no alterations, which suggest that the MGB's styling was 'right' from the word go and examination of Hayter's original quarter-scale drawing, that thankfully survives, confirms this fact. 'Some models may go back half a dozen times. If one is right, then everyone knows it, and it goes straight through,' recalls Don.

Three-quarter rear view of the same mock up. Note the MG badges in the rear light clusters. The two-tone bodywork was finished in blue and white. The design was not proceeded with and Don Hayter took a new EX number and 214/1 became the definitive MGB.

With the MGB's body now confirmed, work went ahead on the new car's choice of power unit. EX 214/2 was a scheme for fitting a V4 two litre engine. This unit, which had been experimentally developed at Longbridge under Dr Duncan Stuart's direction, was also available in V6 form. It was clearly inspired by Lancia experience but while that shallow V had cylinders at 22 degrees to each other, the BMC one had its cylinders at 18 degrees. It had been made in both iron and alloy and the high-placed camshaft was driven by a toothed rubber belt and actuated a BMW type cross pushrod overhead valve layout. There were also thoughts about fitting the V4 version in the MGA, this variation carrying the EX 216 number. The V engine project was eventually abandoned by BMC in view of the enormous investment required to produce it. Also by the early sixties, the Corporation was fully committed to the Alec Issigonis transverse engine front wheel drive theme with the emphasis on space saving and a north/south V engine didn't really fit in with that change of thought. Variation EX 214/3 was for the MGA's Twin Cam engine while 214/4 and /5 were a two litre in-line four created by lopping cylinders three and four from the current BMC C series unit; in fact, Don Hayter's body had been designed around that particular engine. All these schemes were completed by June 1958 though the V4 theme was re-activated in October of that year as 214/6, /7 and /8.

EX 214 in MG parlance and ADO 23 in BMC coding, the first prototype MGB, with unique coil sprung rear axle, almost certainly pictured at Pressed Steel's Cowley factory in 1960. The body was built at Morris Bodies and the car assembled at Abingdon. Finished in silver with green below the feature line, amongst the non-production features were the Triumph Herald sidelights, replaced by purpose-designed ones, windscreen and sill mouldings. It measured 12 feet 8.75 inches overall, one inch shorter than the production cars, on account of its rear suspension.

The prototype's 1588cc MGA engine. Note the twin 1.5 inch H4 SU carburettors and air filters and the absence of an oil cooler which only arrived with the 1798cc engine, and was located in front of the radiator. The engine compartment looks remarkably uncluttered because the wiring loom has yet to be fitted.

But the inevitable financial constraints resulted in the MGB ending up with a production engine. The V4 and the four-cylinder C didn't exist while the twin overhead camshaft unit had developed a reputation for unreliability when used in the Twin Cam version of the MGA. So the B was given the B Series unit which also powered the ZA Magnette saloon from 1953, while it was increased to 1588cc by upping the bore size from 73 to 75mm for the MGA 1600 of 1959. For 1962 came another bore out, to 76mm, the 1600 Mk II MGA having a 1622cc engine. This latter capacity increase was shared with other BMC B Series-powered cars, MG being almost always dependent on the parent Corporation for its changes in engine size.

Don Hayter was also pushing ahead with the design of the B's interior. He styled the facia panel, complete with glove compartment, though the instrumentation layout was largely a carry over from the MGA. One difference was that the horn button was removed from the centre of the facia to the steering wheel hub. Hayter was also responsible for the new aluminium-framed windscreen and the hood and he modified the Austin A40's heater unit for use in the MGB. Seats and trim were designed, respectively, by Jim O'Neill at Abingdon and Eric Carter of Morris Bodies. The seats are particularly noteworthy because the one-piece cushion mouldings were manufactured by Aeropreen Products of High

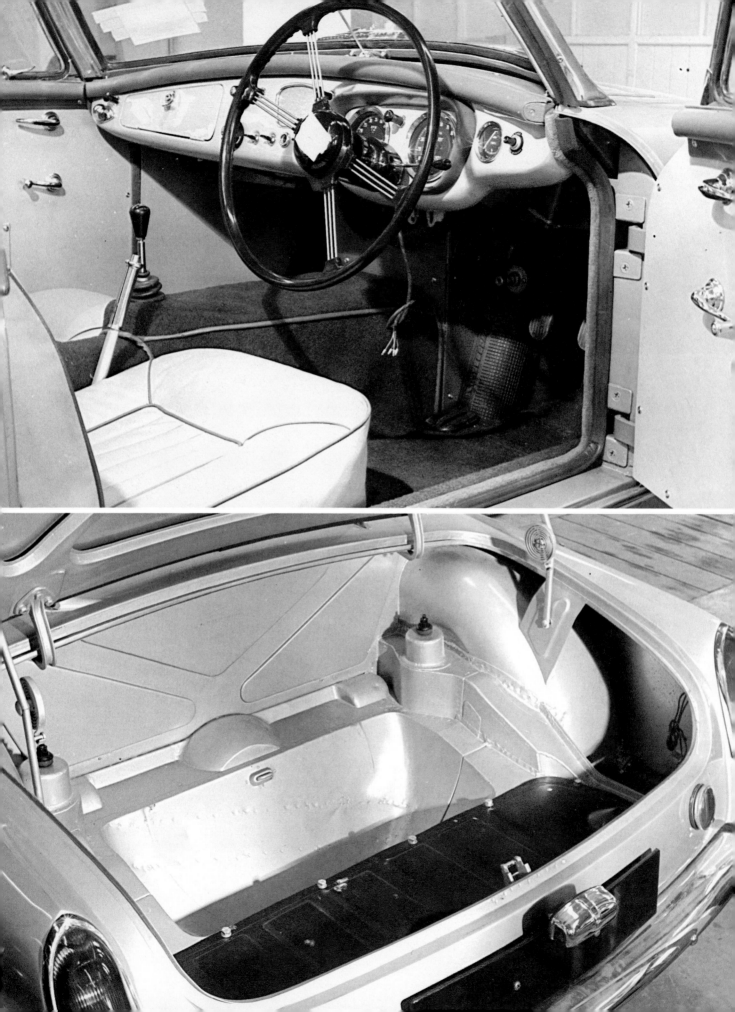

Left: The prototype's dashboard, also the work of Don Hayter. This was a single metal pressing and was a design study he had undertaken for the MGA but never executed. The radio's loud speaker shape was similar to that employed on the Riley 2.6. The dash was considerably modified before it reached production status, as were the door trims and seats. An MGA steering wheel is fitted.

Wycombe, Bucks and the B was one of the first cars to be fitted with them.

By mid-1960 the first MGB prototype was nearing completion. This roadster was finished in a silver upper section and green below the feature line and was very similar to the production car, with the notable exception of the rear suspension. As mentioned earlier, a coil spring/trailing radius arm layout and live rear axle, located by a

Left: The same car's boot, with spare wheel well. Note the diagonal line of welds in the well for a cross-member to locate the Panhard rod mounting, and the shock absorber mountings; the shock absorbers ran in the middle of the coil springs. The cast aluminium boot hinges and return springs were never fitted to the production cars. This car has a purpose-built petrol tank, but when the second prototype with a leaf sprung rear, was built, the 10 gallon MGA tank was reintroduced.

Rear view of the prototype, showing the metal tonneau located behind the front seats. Other differences from the production cars are separate reflectors, later incorporated in the rear light cluster, and Volvo boot lock, while the car is also lacking overriders. Those eventually used on the MGB were produced by Wilmot Breedon, and had been originally designed for another and unrelated car project which did not come to fruition. Also no jacking points have been fitted at this stage.

43

MGB
The illustrated history

Panhard rod, was adopted. At its body end, the rod was attached to the spare wheel mounting. But there were problems. Roy Brocklehurst again: 'With a Panhard rod, you need it to be as long as possible to be effective and its mounting at the chassis end tends to get rather weary. It also has different characteristics on right and left hand corners. We'd already tried out a Watts linkage which was better but expense ruled this out'. So, on this first MGB prototype, not surprisingly, once road testing began, the rod mounting did fracture at the point at which it was attached to the body, though this was corrected by extra reinforcement. Then testers complained that the car seemed to be steering from the back because of the rod's radius of action. There was only one way of resolving the problem cheaply and that was to revert to cart springing which also perpetuated the MGA theme. The leaves were longer than those used on the earlier model, however, and Roy Brocklehurst inclined them in side view to promote a degree of understeer. The only trouble was that this involved lengthening the rear of the car by one inch as the new suspension involved restructuring the boot floor and the extra space was required to permit the spare wheel to lie flat. This meant that Don Hayter had painstakingly to refair every line ahead of the rear wheel arch for a new set of drawings. The MGA's petrol tank was also introduced at this stage.

These revisions required the production of a second prototype, the drawings of which were completed on 26 July 1961. It was finished in red with black upholstery and was fitted with the new cart sprung rear. On this car (there was also a third, created simultaneously) the opportunity was taken to incorporate as many aluminium panels as possible. The MGA's bodies had been produced at Morris Bodies in Coventry and had aluminium doors, bonnet and boot lid. This second experimental MGB incorporated similar features but the idea was dropped on the dual grounds of expense and manufacturing difficulties, though an aluminium bonnet was retained until 1970 on

the production MGB. The third prototype was black painted and red trimmed and came closest to the car that eventually appeared at the 1962 Motor Show. But there was, as yet, no 1622cc engine available so that car was fitted with a 1588cc MGA power unit (number 16GA/U/2259).

Fortunately these last-minute alterations were made before the car's tooling was completed. As we've seen, Pressed Steel was responsible for the manufacture of the MGB's body panels and underframe. The work was carried out, not at Cowley, but at a new plant at Stratton St Margaret, near Swindon, just over 20 miles from Abingdon. Its building had begun in 1956 and, two years later, potential demand was such that the production area was doubled. 'Swindon was tickled pink to have the B. It was really their first complete car, all their other work having been transferred from elsewhere' recalls Don Hayter. Chief engineer at Swindon was Geoffrey Robinson and Dave Osman was put in charge of the MGB project. Roy Brocklehurst also remembers the MGB

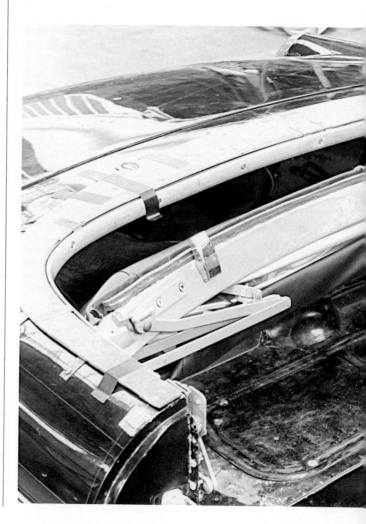

Getting the hood right. This is the packaway type in its raised position being tried out in a prototype car. Note the shaped plywood and aluminium panels which imitate the contours of the window and which have been attached to the door for this exercise.

This is a very interesting photograph as it shows no less than *two* sets of hood frames! In the foreground is the packaway hood, which was supplied with the car. The hoops were split in the middle and stored in the boot when not in use. The hood in the lowered position was never fitted in a production MGB ...

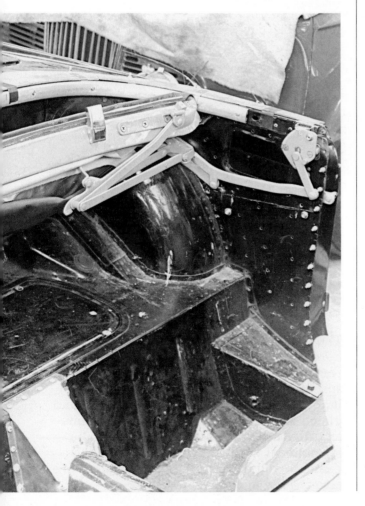

... and was supplied by Hallam, Sleigh and Cheston of Birmingham, though the hood hailed from their factory at Maidenhead, Berkshire. The car is the third, and final prototype MGB, with black bodywork and, eventually, red upholstery.

Right: The engine compartment, minus engine but complete with gearbox. The universal-jointed steering column of this left-hand drive car can be seen as can the twin exhaust pipes: the MGA, by contrast, only had a single pipe.

A series of photographs of a pre-production MGB taken to familiarise the Abingdon production experts with the car's construction. Here the all important angle for engine and gearbox fitting is being gauged though this is an experimental engine, complete with starting handle dog.

as the first job, from start to finish, carried out at Swindon. 'There were plenty of ex-aircraft people in the drawing office who'd been made redundant by Armstrong Whitworth and these loftsmen were very good at drawing complex shapes'. By May 1960, Pressed Steel had a complete breakdown of the B's body and underframe components and started releasing drawings for their own production.

The MGB's robust construction is apparent here with one of the bolt-on front wings removed to reveal the independent front suspension. The coil and wishbone independent front suspension and rack and pinion steering was substantially the same as that used on the MGA. Knock-off hubs for optional wire wheels are fitted to this example and the Lockheed disc brakes are also readily apparent.

As the MGB was fitted with 14 inch wheels, rather than the 15 inch ones of the MGA, it meant that the front disc brakes had to be reduced in size, from 11 to 10.75 inches. The dust cover on the inside of the disc, to prevent stones and road dirt reaching its face and so subjecting the disc pad to undue wear, was another departure from previous practice.

Inset right: The finalised dashboard, unbolted from the bulkhead revealing the flanges used to secure it. The design of the steering wheel still had to be resolved, production cars being fitted with a third set of spokes. Also the radio speaker console still has to be completed.

Inset left: The same car's boot, though lacking a lid, containing the optional stowaway hood, so allowing the maximum of storage space behind the driver. The spare wheel is now located on the floor.

After three prototype MGBs had been completed, a batch of eight pre-production cars were built and this is one of them, photographed at BMC's Cowley studio at the end of 1961. This is virtually identical to the production car and the oil cooler can just be seen through the radiator grille. Note the absence of front overriders, they were initially an optional extra.

Rear view of the same car, with the hood raised, to all intents and purposes the finished product and all ready for manufacture.

When it had come to negotiating the contract for the MGB's tooling, John Thornley had naturally been anxious to keep costs down and, after some rather protracted negotiations, managed to get the bill reduced from £628,000 to £280,000 but an extra £2 was added to the cost of each body. 'Had I known at the time that the B was going to run to over half a million, then that was bad business!' But, then it was expected that the new car would be replaced, at most, by 1970.

There was one last and crucial change to the car's specification before the design was finalised. As we've seen, the MGB was to have been fitted with the 1622cc B Series engine, then current in the MGA 1600 Mk 11 and similar to that fitted to a host of other BMC B Series engined vehicles. Contemporary BMC literature issued to its distributors makes reference to a *1961* MGB powered by an engine with a 16GD prefix (indicating 1622cc). But, as the B was half a hundredweight heavier, at 2072lbs kerb weight, than the MGA, its performance would have been inferior. The A's top speed was just in excess of 100 mph and the fastest speed

A left-hand drive pre-production model, with the dashboard in place though with minor details unresolved. The design of the radio loudspeaker has still to be finalised, though, the interior is complete.

attained by a 1622cc MGB prototype had been around the 94 mph mark. Fortunately for MG, at Longbridge there had been an alteration to the mechanical specification of ADO 17 which was to emerge as the Austin 1800 in 1964. Originally it had been powered by the proposed V4 engine but when this project was discontinued, the B Series four was substituted and its capacity stretched to 1800cc by upping the bore from 76 to 80mm.

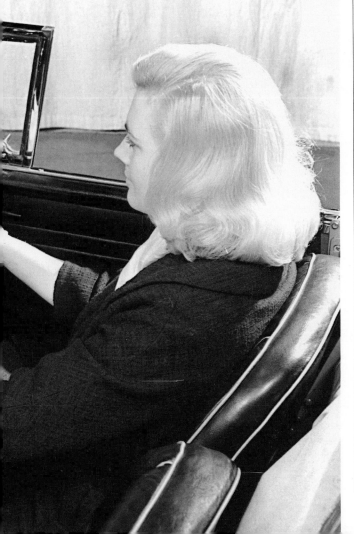

Right-hand drive pre-production MGB, similar to the previous car but fitted with optional Radiomobile radio and ashtray (another MGA inheritance) just ahead of the loudspeaker. Note that this car is fitted with an overdrive; the switch can be seen on the extreme right of the dashboard. MG was experimenting with the D type Laycock unit but this would not be available as an optional extra on production cars until January 1963.

Overleaf: The MGB in all its glory and all set for production. This example is fitted with the optional attached folding hood. John Thornley, Syd Enever, Roy Brocklehurst, Don Hayter and the Abingdon team had produced an outstanding car. Now all it had to do was to sell.

Previous page: The 1798cc version of the BMC B Series engine, as fitted in the MGB, and unique to a BMC car until the arrival of the Austin 1800 in 1964. The capacity increase was achieved by upping the bore size from 76mm to 80mm though this meant siamezing the bores. The oil cooler pipes have been disconnected on this unit. The exhaust side of the 1798cc engine, with twin 1.5 inch HS4 SU carburettors, though not yet fitted with their Cooper air filters. This is an experimental engine. No production cars were fitted with a starting handle dog. Like the previous engine, lifting lugs have been added. Note the cranked gear lever; by contrast, the MGA had a straight one though it operated via a remote control, but because the MGB driver sat further forward in the car, the lever engaged directly with the selector rods.

A familiar but important picture. The arrival of the 100,000th MGA, finished in gold, with cream upholstery, was announced in March 1962 and this celebration picture, staged outside the service department, shows Syd Enever at the wheel and John Thornley on his left. Behind the car is Henry Edward Cecil (Cec) Cousins, another Abingdon stalwart, who joined Morris Garages in 1920 and became MG's works manager in 1944. The car is a Mark 11 version of the MGA, introduced in June 1961 and powered by an enlarged 1622cc engine. It is instantly identifiable by its distinctive recessed radiator grille and badges just behind the air intakes on the front wings but, in this instance, they also read *100,000*. Note the lack of external door handles. The MGA was the last MG sports car to be fitted with a starting handle. Soon after this photograph was taken the car was exported to America for display at the 1962 New York Show. But, as John Thornley points out, MGA sales were beginning to slip from 1959. The MGB did not arrive a moment too soon!

The MGB was to benefit from this capacity increase ahead of the saloon but by the time that it reached production the power unit had been redesigned to incorporate a five-bearing crankshaft, a refinement that also extended to the B.

So, by early 1962, ADO 23 was inching towards a launch date of 20 September, just prior to the London Motor Show. It had not arrived a moment too soon. MGA production had fallen off badly in 1961 with a total of 6085 cars made that year, compared with 16,981

manufactured in 1960. All BMC sports car production had been concentrated at Abingdon from late 1957, the ZB Magnette (the ZA's successor) and Riley 1.5 saloons being transferred to Cowley and Longbridge respectively to make way for the Austin Healey 100 Six. Its smaller first cousin, the 'frog eyed' Sprite went into production at Abingdon in the following year. An MG version, the Midget, appeared in 1961. But output was still running light so, from 1960 until 1963 10,967 Morris Minor Travellers were made at Abingdon and 9147 Minor vans in the 1960/63 period with quality well up to the usual MG standards. A further 3049 MGAs were built in March 1962 and that month witnessed the production of the 100,000th example. By the time manufacture ceased in July the total MGA production figure stood at 101,081 (pushrod 98,970, Twin Cam 2111). It was, at the time, the best selling sports car in the world.

MGB
The illustrated history

As the first production MGB was built on 22 May 1962 (chassis number G-HN3 102) there was a two month overlap with the MGA. This first MGB was an Iris Blue roadster, inevitably left-hand drive, with G-HN3 101, a right-hand drive example, completed six days later on 28 May. Neither car left Abingdon until July and apart from one further right-hander, the first 500 cars were built for the all important American market. A breakdown can be seen opposite of the first MGBs built in 1962.

A sectioned right-hand drive car featured on MGs 1962 Motor Show stand but the visitors who so enthusiastically crowded around it could hardly have guessed that they were looking at the last completely new MG sports car.

Right: **Another view of ADO 34, with MGA-type sidescreens. The front also closely resembled that of the MGB and can be seen more clearly on the extreme left behind the car. A coupé derivative was coded ADO 35 while the Austin Healey version of the open car was ADO 36. Longbridge also produced its own ADO 34, with an 80 inch wheelbase, and body styled by Pininfarina.**

Effectively a scaled down MGB, with a similar detachable metal tonneau, EX 220, better known as ADO 34, was a front wheel drive sports car based on Mini components, built in 1959. Intended as the new MG Midget, it was styled at Abingdon by Dennis Williams and had an 84 inch wheelbase. It was vetoed by Alec Issigonis in 1960 on the grounds that it took little account of the space-saving advantages of the transverse engine location. However, the rear end was transferred to the Austin Healey Sprite-based MG Midget of 1961.

Analysis of the first Year's Production

Chassis nos between:	101 600	601 1100	1101 1600	1601 2100	2101 2600	2601 3100	3101 3600	3601 4100	4101 4600	4601 5100	5101 5500	Total month
May	12											12
June	138											138
July	181											181
August	167	210										377
September	2	288	249	13								552
October		2	241	376	93							712
November			10	111	407	464	374	9				1375
December						36	126	488	430	161	6	1247
January									70	339	494	–

The above gives a total for 1962 of 4,594 cars

Chassis number spans in individual months were as follows:

May	101	–	128
June	103	–	256
July	238	–	447
August	351	–	996
September	537	–	1737
October	812	–	2311
November	1439	–	3795
December	2426	–	5138
January from		4121 on	

this table indicates the chassis numbers of first and last car to be commenced each month

Abingdon production control department counted a total of 4518 cars for 1962; that figure is 76 higher than that shown above compiled by Anders Clausager, the British Motor Industry's Heritage Trust's archivist. Throughout he has used dates when a given car *commenced* build. MG production control may have counted the cars at a later stage of the build process or may have added totals for working weeks in the year, which could mean that the last day or two were counted towards their 1963 figure.

Chapter 2

The MGB *in production 1962-1980*

WHEN THE MGB made its 1962 Motor Show debut it cost £949, had a top speed of around 103 mph, an overall fuel consumption of about 28 mpg and turned the scales at 18.5 cwt making it cheaper, more economical and lighter than the 1.6 litre Sunbeam Alpine, its nearest rival. This Rootes product sold for £956, would touch 98 mph, average 26 mpg and weighed 19.1 cwt. Although the Triumph TR4 had around the same top speed as the B, and accelerated marginally better with its 2.1 litre engine, it was thirstier, £81 more expensive and heavier on account of its separate chassis. Of course, there were faster cars than the MGB but they were all more expensive. The 110 mph Lotus Elan, also launched at the 1962 show, cost £1499 while you would pay out £1190 for the Austin Healey 3000 which was capable of 115 mph plus. And, of course, there was Jaguar's exquisite E-type, capable of 150 mph but costing £2177. In other words John Thornley and Syd Enever had got ADO 23 just about right.

The MGB was roomier and about 2$\frac{1}{2}$ inches wider than its MGA predecessor yet was 3 inches shorter. This was achieved by adopting monocoque construction which allowed Enever to move the toe board and pedals forward by around six inches which meant that the car's occupants sat closer to the engine. In turn, this permitted the creation of a larger boot than the one used on the MGA. There was also room for children to sit behind the seats. Thus the MGB owner could keep his car, even after the arrival of a family, at least until his oldest child was about nine years old. John Thornley even managed to get his four grand children, sitting side by side, in the back of his B!

The integral body/chassis was an immensely strong structure. Its platform was reinforced each side by a deep box section member separated by a metal membrane with the outer section visible as the door sill. The inners were perpetuated by individual members which swept up over the rear axle with the springs shackled to their extremities. At the front of the car, the engine was mounted on two further members that ran forward from a cross-member positioned below the front seats. The double bulkhead was extremely rigid and the front suspension loadings were transferred to it via the longitudinal engine members and the inner wing panels. The scuttle, in its turn, was secured to the transmission tunnel by a fabricated box section, scuttle stiffness being attained by a square section support for the bulkhead from the gearbox cover which also served to contain a loudspeaker when the optional radio was fitted.

The suspension was similar to that used on the MGA but there were important detail differences. In layout the front unit was, in essence, a carry-over though the coil springs were much softer at 73 lb/in compared with the A's 100 lb/in. In addition, the screwed kingpin and bush, as used on the A, was replaced by a plain pin and thrust

Because Abingdon did not begin building the MGB until May 1962, this pre production example was photographed early in 1962 for publicity purposes. It is, inevitably, a left-hand drive example with American number plate mountings. Disc wheels were a standard fitment but these 60 spoke wire wheels had 4$\frac{1}{2}$J rims, rather than the disc's 4J ones, and were available at £34 7s 6d extra.

MGB
The illustrated history

washer. The front suspension had its own rubber-mounted cross-member (this had been welded to the body structure on a prototype but generated excessive noise).

Part of the original colour brochure issued in 1964 to promote the first five-bearing MGB Roadster.

At the rear, the leaves were lengthened by $2\frac{1}{2}$ inches and there were six rather than seven of them. Also softer settings were used on the lever arm rear dampers than those employed on the MGA. The rear axle was basically the same as that used on the A though, because the car's wheels were reduced from 15 to 14 inches in diameter, the final drive ratio was changed from 4.1 to 3.9:1. Four-stud disc wheels with 4J rims were standardised and 5.60-14 Dunlop tyres fitted. A side effect of the smaller wheels was

The definitive MGB shape. This is a 1964 roadster.

SUPERLATIVE in value. 'Superlative' is a word to use with discretion. The 'MGB' meets the challenge with complete confidence. Its forerunner—the 'MGA 1600'—created a record unique in sports-car history with a production of over 100,000. The 'MGB' transcends its redoubtable predecessor in every way. It is built to do so. It has more power, more vivid acceleration, more brisk performance through the gears—consequently more safety; it has more room, more comfort, a superior ride, and more refinements. These advances on a predecessor which itself achieved record success are an impressive indication of the unbeatable value in the 'MGB'. The sports-car connoisseur will find in this car all that he has been looking for.

IN ROAD HOLDING Important contributions to the road-holding properties of the 'MGB' are its chassisless construction, low centre of gravity, wide track, and long wheelbase. Strength through unit construction brings with it the additional advantage of lightness, and consequently more favourable power-to-weight ratio and more effective performance. Independent front-wheel suspension further enhances the comfort of the ride and drive. Disc brakes on the front wheels assure smoothness of operation without brake fade. Rack and pinion steering gives, in true M.G. fashion, a delightful touch to this important aspect of driving. More detailed information on these points will be found in the pages that follow. Quite apart from their individual merit, it is the combination of such features that makes the 'MGB' an unusually delightful car to handle.

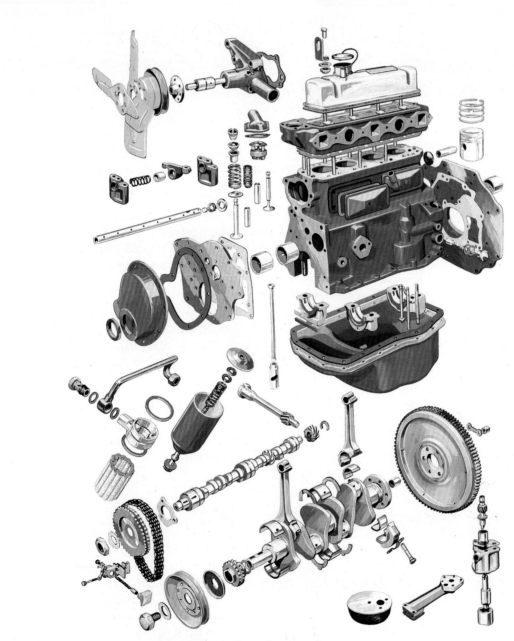

The original three-bearing 1798 cc B-series engine.

that the front Lockheed disc brakes were reduced from 11 to 10³/4 inches diameter while the rear drums remained unchanged. Rack and pinion steering gear was fitted.

Under the bonnet, the MGB's engine looked very similar to the A though the twin HS4 carburettors were fitted with new Cooper paper element filters, said to contribute an extra 3 bhp to the 95 bhp (net) at 5400 rpm the engine developed. The real changes were internal ones, the 1798 cc being attained by increasing the bore size from 76.2 to 80.3 mm while the stroke remained at 88.9 mm. This meant that there was contact between the front and rear pairs of siamesed cylinders, so the gudgeon pin bosses had four rather than two holes to provide additional internal cooling. At the same time the three-bearing crankshaft was considerably stiffened up, with 2¹/8 inch main bearings, in place of the 2 inch ones used previously though their width was reduced by ³/32 to 1¹/8 inches. This allowed the crankshaft webs to be strengthened and thickened by about ¹/16 inch. The big-end bearing size remained the same. A vibration damper, integral with the fan pulley, was added with the intention of increasing timing chain life. The cylinder head was almost identical to that used on the MGA but the compression ratio was reduced from 9 to 8.8:1. This engine capacity, it should be emphasised, was not used in any other BMC

The MGB cost £949, (basic £690, plus £259 purchase tax), on its September 1962 introduction. It was £27 more expensive than the MGA roadster, which sold for £912 in the same year. However, on 5 November purchase tax on cars was reduced from 45 to 25 per cent and the MGB's price came down to £834.

car until the arrival of the Austin 1800 in 1964.

The gearbox with synchromesh on second, third and top gears also perpetuated the MGA theme though bottom was slightly lower at 14.21 instead of 15.65 overall. Because the driver sat further forward in the B than the A, a remote gear lever was not necessary so the control fed straight into the box which resulted in a more positive change. The car's interior was well finished, the new, wider seats having leather wearing surfaces, though one needed a spanner to slacken off the securing nut to adjust them for rake. Leather cloth was used for the squab edges and the matching door trim. The dashboard was black crackle finished and there was a new, three-spoke steering wheel with the MG octagon at its centre. The eight-sided theme was echoed on the radio loudspeaker grille. Weather protection was good with winding windows and quarter lights and there were two alternative hoods available. The standard

Underbonnet view of the 1967 MGB, which has been fitted with a non-standard brake servo.

The roadster's driving compartment, complete with original ashtray, which was an optional extra.

Roger Jerram's 1967 MGB roadster.

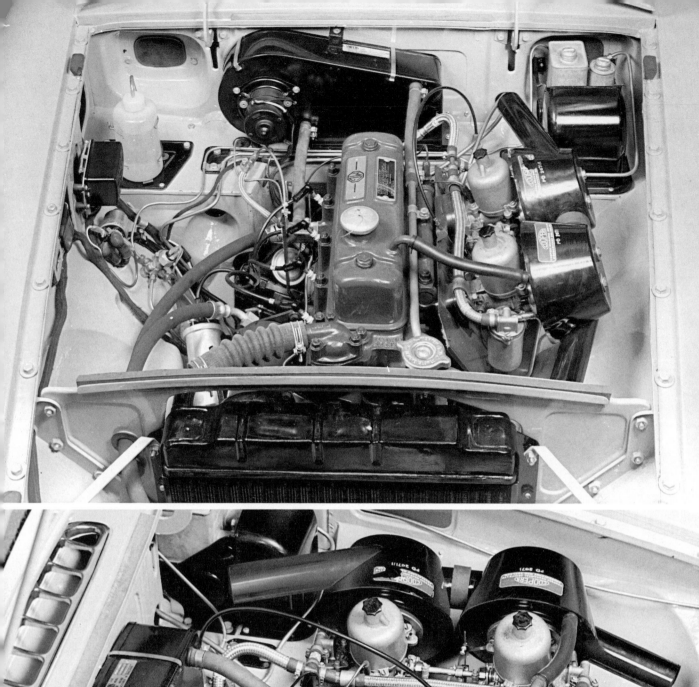

Left: Under the bonnet of the left-hand drive car. The B Series engine, it developed 95 bhp at 5400 rpm, designated type 18G on the model's introduction, closely resembled that of its MGA predecessor though there was considerably more under-bonnet space. Note the pipes running to the optional oil cooler; it cost £18 18s 9d more on cars for the home market but was a standard fitment on the export ones. The Smiths heater followed MGA precedent and was also available at extra cost, and was £16 16s more. 'In fact it was a nuisance to build a car without a heater,' recalls Thornley, 'but we made it an extra to keep the overall price of the car down'. It drew in air from the grille mounted directly above.

Left: The offside of the engine of a 1962 MGB. It is virtually identical to that of its MGA predecessor. Like all Austin overhead valve engines, the electrics (distributor, dynamo and starter motor) were all well away from the inlet and exhaust manifolds. This is, incidentally, engine number 1853-1.

one had a detachable folding frame, with a separate cover, that could be stowed in the boot. This had the advantage of leaving the rear of the cockpit clear. The alternative De Luxe version, which cost an extra £5 10s, was not detachable and folded down behind the seats. Also available at extra cost was the heater which was another £16 16s 11d.

By the time that the MGB went into production, Abingdon was responsible only for the car's assembly. No manufacturing took place, as had been the case with the MGA. The MGB bodies started out life at the Pressed Steel Company's plant near Swindon and were transported by road to the BMC Morris Bodies Branch at Quinton Road, Coventry. A brand new paint shop had been built there to accommodate the B and a dip system was introduced for applying the primer. Then came the spray painting with each coat rubbed down by hand; the body was then trimmed and the seats and carpets allotted to their respective hulls but not secured in place. Next, six at a time, the shells were transported south again to Abingdon. They were then taken to the upper trim deck of the main assembly shop where the facia panel and instruments were fitted and seats and carpeting secured. Once completed, the body was lowered by a hoist through a hole in the floor where it picked up its suspension, rear axle and steering gear.

An MGA engine shown for comparative purposes looking, by contrast, very cramped. The most obvious differences are the twin SU carburettors. The A employed 1.5 inch H4 units, with gauze air filters, while the B's engine was fitted with their HS4 derivatives with Cooper air filters and renewable paper elements.

The front wishbones and shock absorbers had been previously delivered direct to Abingdon by component suppliers, in the latter instance, Armstrong. The front hub and Lockheed disc brake assemblies came from the BMC Tractors and Transmissions plant at Ward End, Birmingham which was the old Wolseley car factory. John Thompson Pressing supplied the front suspension cross-member while the rack and pinion steering came from Cam Gears. The rear axle, complete with brakes, was also delivered from T and T's at Ward End.

MGB Mark 1 roadster, Type G/HN3, 1962-1967

Engine
Cylinders: 4
Bore: 80.26 mm
Stroke: 88.9 mm
Displacement: 1798 cc
Valves: Pushrod/overhead
Compression ratio: 8.8:1
Carburettors: Twin SU 1.5 in type HS4
Power output: 95 bhp at 5400 rpm

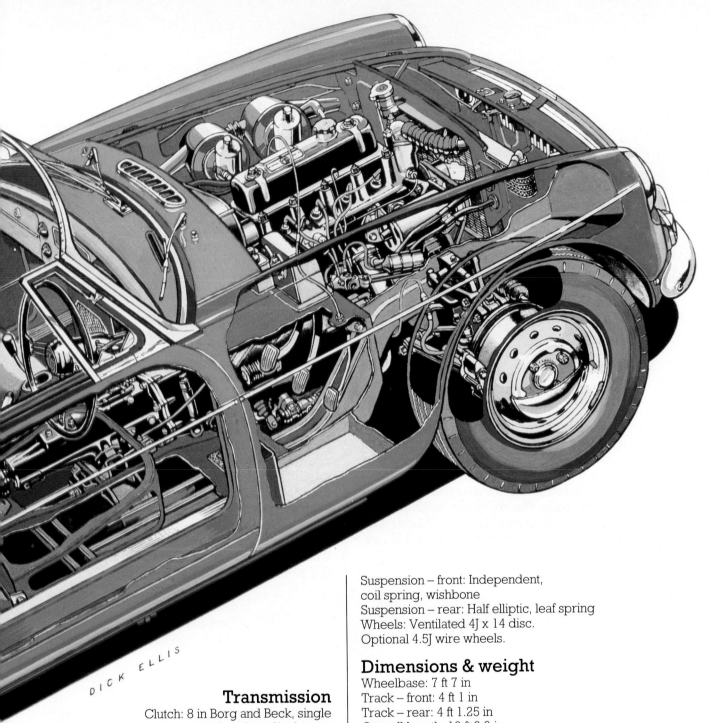

DICK ELLIS

Transmission

Clutch: 8 in Borg and Beck, single
dry-plate diaphragm
Gearbox: 4-speed, synchromesh on 2nd,
3rd and top gears
Ratios: Top 1.0, 3rd 1.37, 2nd 2.21, 1st 3.64,
reverse 4.76
Overdrive: Optional from January 1963, Laycock
Type D, Top .80, 3rd 1.10
Final drive: 3.9:1

Chassis

Construction: Unitary
Brakes:Lockheed
Front: 10.75 in disc
Rear: 10 x 1.75 in drum
Steering: Rack and pinion, 3 turns lock to lock

Suspension – front: Independent,
coil spring, wishbone
Suspension – rear: Half elliptic, leaf spring
Wheels: Ventilated 4J x 14 disc.
Optional 4.5J wire wheels.

Dimensions & weight

Wheelbase: 7 ft 7 in
Track – front: 4 ft 1 in
Track – rear: 4 ft 1.25 in
Overall length: 12 ft 9.2 in
Overall width: 4ft 11.9 in
Overall height: 4 ft 1.4 in
Ground clearance: 4.5 in
Turning circle: 32 ft
Kerb weight: 18.5 cwt

Performance

Maximum speed: 103 mph
Acceleration: 0-60 mph 12.2 secs
Overall fuel consumption: 22 mpg

Production

Deliveries: USA, 71,722; UK, 19,420;
Rest of world, 18,720; total 115,898

The dashboard of a left-hand drive car though still fitted wth the experimental two-spoke steering wheel. The layout is virtually a mirror image of the right-hand drive one, with the windscreen wiper sweeps reversed, while the floor mounted dip switch is on the extreme left of the pedal controls. The direction indicator tell tails above the rev counter and speedometer are also different on this car.

The right-hand drive MGB dashboard in its finished form. Overdrive has yet to appear and, when available, the switch would be located next to the petrol gauge just to the right of the steering wheel which has finally received its third set of spokes though there are just two of them. The ashtray cost an extra £1 7s 6d. The map reading lamp, inherited from the MGA, could be operated when the side lights were switched on. The winders indicate the presence of wind up windows.

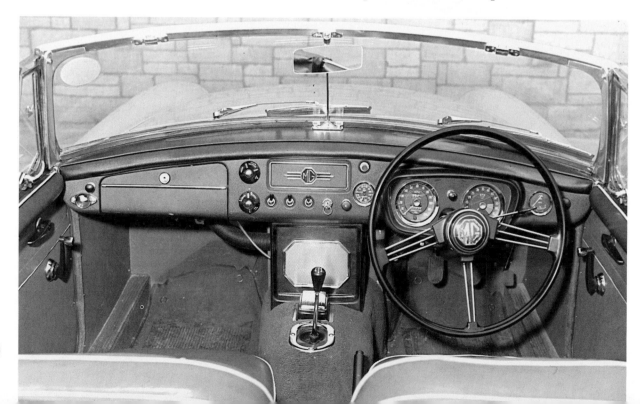

The distinctive positioning of the MGA
steering wheel spokes echoed those of the
EX 179 record breaker of 1957, a feature
which was also perpetuated on EX 181.
Also the horn button is in the middle of the
A's dashboard. It was more conventionally
located in the centre of the steering wheels
on the MGB.

Two small children, or one transversely
mounted adult, could be carried behind
the seats and a tailor-made cushion was
available at extra cost. The space could
alternatively be used for luggage though
might mostly be taken up by the folding, as
opposed to the packaway, hood when it
was furled. The carpeted base is
removable to gain access to the two 58
amp hour six volt batteries, wired in series
and located each side of the propeller
shaft, a less than desirable MGA
inheritance.

The MGB's seats were adjustable and the wearing surfaces finished in leather while the sides and back, along with the doortrim, were made of matching leathercloth. Although rake was adjustable, this could only be achieved by repositioning a nut with the appropriate spanner.

The MGB's boot, as supplied with the tool kit secured by a strap with the jack and wheelbrace to the left of the spare wheel. These items, in truth, took up much of the space.

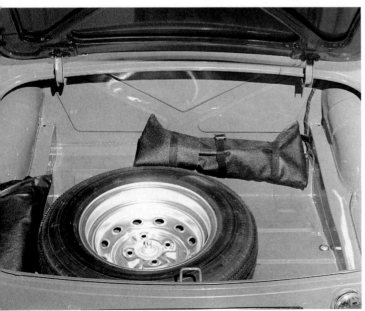

Next came the fitment of the engine and gearbox. This derived from BMC's Long-bridge factory and the power unit came complete with its electrics. But there was a small preparation line at Abingdon where the engine was dressed with its special MG inlet and exhaust manifolding and twin SU carburettors. Finally, the road wheels went on. MG received wheels and tyres separately from Dunlop and united them there.

After assembly, the cars were then started and test driven the six miles to Marcham village and back. If this proved satisfactory, the car was ready for dispatch. If not, it was returned to the factory for rectification. There were minor changes to this procedure during the MGB's 18 year production life. The arrival of the GT in 1965 saw Abingdon, for a time, undertake its trimming though this was only carried out for a fairly short period. It is interesting to note, however, that the Austin Healey Sprite and MG Midget *were* trimmed at the factory. Then, in 1971, the BMC Bodies Branch in Coventry closed and Cowley took over the car's painting and trimming which made far more geographical sense. The road testing was also later discontinued in favour of roller running.

The MGB's first full production year was 1963 when 23,308 roadsters were built. It was a record MG output for Abingdon and 1964 was even better with 26,542 cars manufactured. That year's Motor Show witnessed the arrival of the Austin 1800 saloon and although its engine shared the MGB's 1798 cc capacity, the sports car's three-bearing crankshaft was not regarded as being sufficiently refined for a passenger car. Consequently the bottom end was redesigned and a five-bearing crankshaft introduced which meant finding room for two extra bearings. This was achieved without affecting the external dimensions of the power unit. A departure from previous practice was the fitment of symetrically divided big-end caps; previously they had been split at an angle. Nineteen-sixty-five model year Bs were therefore fitted with the new engine. Because of the extra bearings, it didn't rev quite as freely as the earlier unit, but this was more than offset by the more robust bottom end, the earlier three-bearing crankshaft having suffered from occasional breakages after prolonged use.

The MGB has the characteristic of looking good from any angle from which it is photographed. The boot is lockable, with the same key used for the glove compartment. A different one was employed for starting which also locked both doors.

Left: The underside of the MGB. This car is fitted with the optional front anti-roll bar (standardised in November 1966) while the banjo-type rear axle inherited from the MGA, which endured on the roadster until April 1967, can also be seen.

An American specification B, with standard four-stud disc wheels and the hood raised. It is visually identical to its right-hand drive equivalent, with the exception of the

Left: A left-hand drive 1962 MGB all set for the American market, complete with optional wire wheels and white wall tyres. Although this car appears to be lacking a badge, the example fitted was one of a batch supplied to MG which also acted as a reflector – the specification had to be changed!

indicators which are white, the same colour as the side lights, rather than the amber of the British cars.

Left: The left-hand drive car with the hood lowered and a full tonneau cover in position. This was a standard fitting on export cars but was £11 extra on British-sold Bs.

Below left: The same car with the hood raised, showing the excellent rear visibility available. The folding hood cost £5 10s extra. The hood colour depended on the colour of the body; the following combinations applied to pre-1964 cars: Tartan Red body, red hood, red or black interior; Iris Blue/blue/black or blue; Chelsea Grey/grey/red; Old English White/grey/red or black; Black/grey/red or black. Also note the all-red rear lights on this American specification car.

Double page spread: Hereby hangs a tail. The Trident's rear-mounted Rolls-Royce Spey jet engines provide yet another background for this 1962 publicity photograph. Here an MGB is joined by the Cowley-built, front wheel drive MG 1100, a twin carburettor version of the Morris 1100 announced in 1962, at the same time as the MGB. It remained in production until 1971, by which time 143,067 had been built, making it the best-ever selling MG saloon. A Mark II Austin Healey 3000 is on the right; Abingdon built since 1957 it endured until 1967.

Overleaf: One of the original MGB publicity photographs, embargoed until 20 September 1962. The original caption read: 'Modern achievement in two different spheres – the MG series MGB with Britain's newest airliner, the Vickers VC10'. The location is the old Brooklands racing circuit at Weybridge, Surrey, where the aircraft was built, and the track where MG cars had performed with distinction in pre-war days.

Left: A pre-production American specification MGB; the centre of attention on both land and water! The windscreen surround is of polished aluminium and therefore maintenance free. The MGA, by contrast, had a chrome-plated surround.

Right: An MGB in an appropriate setting, a 1962 car amongst the gliders at Kidlington airfield, near Oxford, fully equipped with optional fog and spot lamps, wire wheels and radio.

Below: Another 1962 publicity photograph, this time a right-hand drive car with optional wire wheels. The MGB's attraction to the female sex was a theme that was to be featured continually in MG's publicity material.

The same car as above at speed with the hood raised. Although the MGB was a 100 mph car, it was much more of a high-speed tourer than a sports car, which considerably broadened its appeal amongst the public.

MGB
The illustrated history

Top: Autocar published its first road test of an MGB roadster in its issue of 26 October 1962. The magazine achieved a mean top speed of 103.2 mph in this example, registered 523 CBL, and commented that, 'For owners of the MGA, one of the great joys of the model has always been its tidy, sure footed and easily controllable handling ... and the new MGB is even better. There is slight understeer until the limit of adhesion is approached, when the rear wheels begin to gently break away. The response to steering correction is immediate, and at speed on twisting country roads, the MG is most satisfying to handle'. This test car was fitted with a Smiths 'all-transistor Radiomobile receiver' while the 'comfortable and softly padded seats ... give good support in the small of the back and right under the thighs, as well as holding the occupants securely in fast cornering'. Note the raised driver's window, locking latch on the edge of the passenger's door and optional seat belts. The MGB was photographed at the rear of the magazine's offices at Dorset House, Stamford Street in London SE1. (Courtesy Quadrant/Autocar)

Centre: The engine of *Autocar's* test car, fitted with a heater and oil cooler, which were available at extra cost. The magazine considered under-bonnet accessibility good, apart from that of the distributor made difficult by the oil cooler pipes. (Courtesy Quadrant/Autocar)

Bottom: In June 1963, the MGB was offered with this works glass-fibre hardtop, made by Denis Ferranti Laminations of Bangor, North Wales which was available throughout the MGB's manufacturing life. The only other change in specifications by this time was the availability of overdrive, a D type Laycock unit, which operated on third and top gears and cost an extra £60 8s 4d though was not initially available on cars produced for the American market, so as not to damage Austin Healey 3000 sales there.

106 FLY

Previous page: Police 1. A distinctive white MGB, one of a batch run by the Lancashire constabulary with blue wing-mounted lamp, individual spotlight and siren. Police MGBs were often fitted with alternators because of the extra electrical equipment they carried; ordinary production cars were not so equipped until 1967.

Above: Police 2: Women Metropolitan police officers going about their duties in an MGB, pictured on London's Westminster Bridge, with Big Ben in the background. The marque had a long-standing association with the force, the pre-war TA and VA models being the first to be offered in specially equipped police guise.

Opposite top: Another 1963 roadster, with optional spot and fog lamps and radio.

With the MGB firmly established as the fastest selling MG ever produced at Abingdon, John Thornley once again reverted to his original GT theme. 'I wanted to produce a car that no managing director would be ashamed to leave in his car park'. Fortunately its design was pretty well complete before the roadster went into production. It carried the EX 227 designation and MG's Jim Stimson did the conversion. Don Hayter recalls that the quarter-scale model – no actual car was made – was rather like the contemporary Aston Martin. 'And everyone said yes ... but'. It wasn't right, so MG decided to hand the project over to Pininfarina, which had been involved with BMC since the fifties, the Austin A40 of 1958 being the first fruits of the liaison. Farina was instructed to make the minimum of alterations and, when the green GT prototype arrived back at Abingdon, 'we thought it was really super,' Hayter recalls. Farina had, in fact, made remarkably few changes but those they had undertaken were sufficient to tip the aesthetic scales and the result was sensational. One of the main differences

between the Abingdon GT and the Pininfarina one was that the Italian styling house had increased the height of the windscreen by two inches over the roadster and the Turin maestros also contributed feature lines which added an extra crispness to the car's appearance. The strength of the conversion was that it didn't look like one and consequently the GT retains its own very individual character. Once he'd seen the prototype, John Thornley was naturally anxious to get it into production as soon as possible.

Fortunately for MG, Pininfarina was one of the first stylists to adopt computer-assisted design, so Abingdon received full-size body sections on Mylar plastic film which were quickly turned into Pressed Steel production drawings at Swindon. Although roadster panels were used as far as possible, the GT demanded some special ones of its own. These were mainly to cater for the larger windscreen and roof and there were changes to the body structure to permit the fitment of occasional seats which also folded flat. A hinged tailgate completed an intensely practical design.

The tourer's manufacturing process was repeated for the GT though, as already noted, the first ones were trimmed by MG rather than the Coventry Bodies Branch. With the announcement of the new model at the 1965 Motor Show, *Motor* impishly commented: 'Taking a firm grasp of the alphabet, BMC have announced the MBG GT'. It was priced at just under the £1000 mark at £998 which was £144 more than the roadster. *Autocar* enthused that it was 'perhaps one of the prettiest sports coupés ever to leave the BMC drawing boards,' which, although not strictly accurate, summed up the general mood. Mechanically the GT was almost identical to the open car though a front anti-roll bar, optional on the roadster, was made standard and the rear springs were uprated to cope with the additional weight. The only major difference was the fitment of a Salisbury-type rear axle, produced by BMCs Tractors and Transmissions division. When the MGB had gone into production it had used the MGA banjo unit and there had been noise problems. These, fortunately, hadn't been so

Created by Jacques Coune of Brussels, the Berlinette MGB 1800 was launched at that city's Motor Show in January 1964. The car was metal to the rear of the doors; thereafter the roof, sides and boot lid were glass-fibre with a new box section welded between the rear wheel arches. The interior was retrimmed and the boot enlarged with access from the car's interior. Mechanically standard, with the exception of an Abarth exhaust system (Coune was an agent), the car was priced at 180,000 Belgian francs (£1285). By June, Coune was claiming to be producing 12 to 15 examples a month and was looking for a British constructor to undertake assembly of four a month. However, the arrival of the MGB GT in October 1965, neatly undercut the Berlinette and only 58 examples were built. This particular example (chassis no G/HN3 36122) is thought to be the first production Berlinette. It was built for Walter Oldfield, general manager of the Nuffield Press (1935-1965). With the help of MG, in 1963 he supplied Coune with a roadster, stripped of its trim, and it was returned to him in April 1964. It attracted considerable attention. Not only did MG's Syd Enever borrow it for evaluation but it was also driven by BMC's chairman

George Harriman and president Lord Lambury (formerly Sir Leonard Lord). Oldfield kept the car until 1979 when it was bought by Mike Akers; it is featured in colour on page 91.

noticeable on the A, with its separate chassis, but when it was transferred to the MGB with its monocoque structure, the shortcoming became more apparent. This would have been even more obvious on the closed GT which was why the more robust Salisbury unit, that absorbed far more of its self-generated noise, was introduced. The roadster, however, continued with its banjo casing until 1967 when the Salisbury unit was made common to both models.

A 1964 MGB, still costing £834, with hardtop, its colour/body combinations being set down by the factory. They are: Tartan Red, Old English White, Black body/grey or red hardtop; Iris Blue/blue. From the 1964 model year, Chelsea Grey was discontinued as a body colour and replaced by British Racing Green, which was offered with a grey or black hood, a black interior and black or Old English White hardtop.

The 1965 MGB: a left-hand drive car shown here, intended for the European market, identifiable by the side lights adjacent to the radiator rather than on the outer edge of the units. Apart from this minor difference, the car is virtually unchanged externally since 1962. Under the bonnet, however, was a five-bearing crankshaft version of the B Series engine, shared with

the newly introduced Austin 1800. The standard engine had an 8.8:1 compression ratio but 8:1 was available on export cars, which developed 91 bhp at 5400rpm.

Left: The five-bearing crankshaft MGB engine, introduced in October 1964, was virtually identical to its three-bearing predecessor and the oil cooler was standardised at the same time. The power unit was redesignated 18 GB. The gearbox was fitted with an enlarged first motion shaft, while the starter motor was also altered.

Below: MGBs were often seen on the streets of Abingdon when they were driven to the town's railway station for dispatch by train. However, this 1965 photograph, showing an MGB roadster on trade plates and a similarly attired MG Midget and Austin Healey Sprite, are going in the wrong direction, so perhaps they are being

Left: A Downton conversion on an MGB. Note the crankcase breather, introduced on the *three*-bearing engine in February 1964 (18 GA) with the crankcase breather valve located on top of the rocker box. The Downton changes included a modified cylinder head, 9.3:1 compression ratio, different camshaft, fabricated three-branch exhaust pipe and twin 1.75 inch SUs on a special manifold which cost £97. These contributed to a top speed of 112 mph, approximately six mph faster than the standard car, with improved acceleration to match.

driven for the benefit of the photographer! This is Abingdon High Street with the town's famous town hall, completed in 1682, and designed by Christopher Kempster, a pupil of Sir Christopher Wren, in the background. Up until the mid 1970s, when roller testing took over, MGBs were road tested prior to dispatch but the two mile run took them through open country rather than the town. Minor adjustments were then made. There was also a longer 4.8 mile route when items such as water temperature, axle noise, brakes and so forth were evaluated.

MGB
The illu

The MGB GT, as introduced in October 1965, arguably one of the best looking British cars of the decade. These original BMC publicity photographs were taken in the grounds of Blenheim Palace, which is only 14 miles from Abingdon.

Still looking good after 24 years, this 1964 MGB Berlinette 1800 by Jacques Coune is the car featured in black and white on page 86. Today it is owned by Mike Akers.

Another Coune bodied MGB. This left hand drive example was pictured at an MG Car Club meeting in 1977. About 12 examples of the original 58 are thought to exist. (Courtesy Piers J.S. Hubbard)

The MGB GT, introduced in October 1965, cost £998, which was £143 more than the open model which price by then had risen to £855. It also weighed 251 lb more, an increase from 2128 lb to 2379 lb. Its arrival represented the expression of John Thornley's concept that a closed MGB would be one which 'no managing director would be ashamed to leave in his car park'. Slightly slower than the roadster, its extra weight was offset by its improved aerodynamics though acceleration was slower, the GT was to remain in production until 1980. This is the first car to be produced, following the arrival of the Pininfarina built prototype. Abingdon, Britain and Turin, Italy had combined to produce this well-proportioned, functional shape. Note the small *MGB GT* badge on the tailgate which was soon enlarged.

Opposite, top left: Unlike the roadster, where the spare wheel was exposed in the boot, in the GT it was neatly concealed beneath the carpeted floor, along with the jack.

Opposite, top right: The GT's carrying capacity was a great improvement on that of the roadster. The storage space was 3 feet 2 inches wide and 2 feet 6 inches from front to rear, available with the rear seat in place. When the back was lowered, the carrying capacity became positively palatial by MG standards, to 3 feet 2 inches square.

Right: The principal mechanical difference between the GT and roadster was that the closed car was fitted with this quieter Salisbury-type rear axle though the roadster continued until 1967 with the ex-MGA banjo unit, as its shortcomings were not so apparent. The GT's rear suspension was stiffer than the open car's because it was more tail heavy, but as this increased oversteer, an anti-roll bar was fitted on the front. The 100 lb front springs were also stiffer than the roadster's, which by 1965 had 90 lb coils. Note the battery boxes; the twin six volt batteries would survive until 1975.

MGB
The illustrated history

Not surprisingly, weight went up with the GT. By 1965 the roadster weighed 2128 lb and the GT was 251 lb heavier at 2379 lb. Also, acceleration was slightly down, but the GT in its original form was capable of just over 100 mph. Fuel consumption was also marginally lower with an overall consumption figure of 26 mpg, compared with the open car's 28. By the end of 1965, 524 GTs had left Abingdon and in 1966, the first full year of production, 10,241 were manufactured. The same year roadster production dipped somewhat to 22,675 but, of course, overall MGB output was up to 32,916. GTs continued to be built until the

Bernard Rengger owns this 1967 GT and completely restored it over a two and half year period.

The pristine engine compartment of the Rengger GT.

end of the B's 18 year production run and, eventually, about a quarter of all Bs made were closed cars.

Had the MGB ceased production in 1970 this is the car that would have replaced it. Designated EX 234 in the MG design register, it would have also taken the place of the long running Austin Healey based MG Midget.

The GT's door trim was also virtually identical to that of the roadster though the driver's door has acquired a pocket because of the relative inaccessibility of the glove compartment.

The GT's 'office'. The heater was a standard fitting though, amazingly, it was still an optional extra on the roadster and remained so until the 1969 model year. Note that the seat backrest rake adjustment was still possible only by relocating the bolt at the base of the seat with the aid of the appropriate spanner.

Unlike the open car, the GT had a proper rear seat where two small children could be accommodated, making the car a real attraction to the family man and was also sufficiently well-mannered for his wife to drive. The nut at the base of the transmission tunnel is for the provision of seat belts.

The daughter of MG's engine build foreman, Jimmy Cox, demonstrates the limitations of the GT's rear passenger accommodation. Interior trim was either black or, as in this case, red, depending on the body colour.

MG's hard working ERX 498C pictured in the pits at Silverstone in the autumn of 1965 when it served as a course car.

This is the car, registered EOJ 221C, featured in *Motor*'s road test of 19 February 1966. 'The performance of the GT is little worse than its soft topped brother', the magazine reported. 'The 0-60 mph time is 13.2 secs, compared with 12.6 secs for the open car, and although the GT begins to fall behind further up the speed range, with a 0-90 mph time of 35.8 secs, instead of 30.9, the maximile speed ... is virtually the same at 103.3 mph, in place of 102.8 mph, probably because at speeds above 90 mph, the lower drag of the GT takes effect'. However, *Motor* was critical of the car's ride as there was 'a good deal of pitch over rough surfaces' and the seats 'which few of our staff found comfortable'. (Courtesy Motor)

The driving compartment of the same car, looking much the same as the roadster of four years before. The only difference is the overdrive switch, to the right of the steering wheel, and also the straight, rather than cranked gear lever. *Motor*'s testers pointed out that while front seat room was adequate, 'the range of seat rake adjustment ... [needed] to be increased'. By this time the passenger had benefited from a floor-mounted cubby hole. (Courtesy Motor)

The increased emphasis that MG was placing on the European market is reflected by these photographs of a 1966 GT, emphasising its carrying capacity. Kilometres per hour speedometers and twin horns were amongst the export options offered.

Only the plates have been changed! What was a Swiss-registered GT in the previous picture has become a German one, with a neutral central-European background.

When the MGB had been conceived, John Thornley had, at most, been thinking in terms of a seven to eight year production life, which would have meant a new MG sports car by around 1970. But he was sufficiently realistic to be aware of the spiralling costs of body tooling and, for this reason, he was convinced that the MGB would probably be Abingdon's last steel-bodied car. He was already thinking in terms of a glass-fibre-bodied MG as a long-term alternative.

But a successor there had to be and, in 1963, a year after the MGB went into production, work started on a new MG sports car with Roy Brocklehurst responsible for its conception. He had been made MG's project engineer in September 1961 and, by the end of 1964, had been appointed assistant chief engineer, and thus became Syd Enever's heir apparent. Designated EX 234, the new car started out life as a replacement for the ageing MG Midget, the body structure of which dated back to the Austin Healey Sprite of 1958. But, as the design evolved, there were strong financial arguments that it should also serve as the MGB's successor. This meant that only one costly set of body tools would be required, rather than two. So although the one and only example was fitted with a 1275cc BMC A Series engine, the under-bonnet space was large enough to accept the larger B Series unit which powered the MGB.

By this time, Brocklehurst and his small development team of Jim Stimson, Mike Holiday and Dave Seymour were operating from the somewhat unlikely surroundings of the MG boiler house. 'I know it sounds terrible but it was a big, new building that, for a time, had only one automatic boiler. There was plenty of room and it was very warm' remembers Roy. He and his team took over half the building and they had a design office there along with a small workshop. 'We were well away from the production line and there was a pleasant outlook over a nearby field'.

When Graham Robson, then a member of *Autocar*'s staff, reported on his drive in this MGB roadster for the magazine's sports car test day, published in its issue of 27 April 1967, he enthused: 'By modern standards . . . [the MGB was] beginning to be a bit too solid and rugged, but in Silverstone's wet and blustery conditions, it felt like the safest car of the day. That boast of "Safety Fast" is not idle.' (Courtesy Quadrant/Autocar)

The roadster received this Salisbury rear axle in April 1967, so bringing it into line with the GT. From cars G-HN3 123716 to 132922, either could be fitted. The 12 gallon petrol tank had been introduced in March 1965 and replaced the original MGA type which was secured, somewhat unsatisfactorily because they succumbed to rusting, by metal straps. This later tank is retained by nine bolts.

Both the roadster and GT were fitted with reversing lights from April 1967, which automatically lit when reverse gear was engaged. The change came on the roadster, at chassis number 128801, body number 100414, and on the GT at chassis number 139824, body number 016928.

Left: Had BMC not been taken over by the Leyland Motor Corporation in 1968, this car, coded EX 234 and designed in 1964, would have probably replaced the MGB *and* Midget in 1970. Roy Brocklehurst was responsible for the creation of two underframes. One was disguised under a light blue Austin Healey Sprite body while the other was dispatched to Pininfarina and this light green roadster was returned to Abingdon in 1968. Hydrolastic all-independent suspension was fitted and although a 1275cc A Series engine is fitted, the B series MGB unit could have been accommodated.

Ex 234's suspension was completely new. Earlier experiments had been carried out with a Mini based Sprite/Midget replacement (ADO 34/35) with Hydrolastic suspension. A similar all independent system applied to 234 and Roy Brocklehurst evolved a layout in conjunction with Alex Moulton, the system's creator. 'Hydrolastic is fine for sports cars, in fact it's better for open cars than saloons where it can produce excessive pitch,' Roy explains, 'but the system we evolved for 234 was completely new and shared no common components with current BMC saloons.' The car featured front and rear wishbones in conjunction with

Left: The other side of EX 234 with the hood up and the nicely sculptured tail shown to effect. Note the push button door locks and lack of the side trim which is fitted to the offside.

EX 234's interior, just a two-plus-two, with black facia and brown upholstery; it was an enormous improvement on the Sprite/Midget, with wind-up windows and quarter-lights in the MGB manner.

MGB
The illustrated history

the interconnected Hydrolastic layout and a chassis mounted differential. The body lines had meanwhile been completed, on 12 February 1964, and these, along with the underframe, were dispatched to Pininfarina. The car that was returned to Abingdon was an outstanding 2 + 2 open two-seater with a neat tail and a front that echoed the MGB. It was a worthy successor but one, alas, that never went into production because the necessary investment was not forthcoming from MG's BMC parent.

Despite the new safety laws, this German bound 1966 MGB roadster has eared hub caps, so perhaps it was built prior to the legislation becoming effective. From the 1966 model year, only black hoods were available on all roadsters, grey and blue having been discontinued.

But by this time MG, and Roy Brocklehurst in particular, was grappling with the results of legislation implemented by the American Motor Vehicle and Road Traffic Act of 1966. As US sales were an integral ingredient of the MGB formula, these safety regulations had an enormous impact on Abingdon and involved MG in costly and time consuming work to modify its car to meet the requirements. The American safety lobby had been spearheaded by Ralph Nader, a young lawyer who, in 1965, had seen the publication of his first book *Unsafe At Any Speed*. The following year came the new Act and headaches for the American car makers and for foreign firms, like MG, which exported a high proportion of their production to the United States. It was intended that the new requirements be progressively introduced from 1 September 1967. Some ambiguity in the drafting of the regulations however, resulted in the American car manufacturers and foreign car importers taking the administration to court. British car makers, in the shape of Roy Brocklehurst, were represented at this hearing and the appellants were given a four month stay of execution, the legislation to apply from 1 January 1968.

The MGB sold in America from the

Problems associated with selling MGBs in America were a continual preoccupation at Abingdon. Here a potential accessory, a bar to protect the B's vulnerable side lights from bumpers of larger and higher American cars, is being evaluated in 1966.

Top left: The MGB was fitted with provision for seat belts from 1962 which were available as an optional extra from the very outset. Here Tom Haig, MG's test driver, displays the conventional diagonal belt. Seat belts were fitted to American specification Bs from the 1968 model year though it was not until 1975 that they were standardised on British-built roadsters. *Top right:* Impending safety legislation in America meant MG preparing its cars to cope with the legal avalanche. Here an American specification B displays the wiped areas of its windscreen wipers, while the second line relates to de-frosting capabilities of its heater.

beginning of 1968 still looked similar to its British counterpart, with the exception of triple windscreen wipers, while wing mounted warning reflectors followed in 1969. The principal differences were only apparent when the bonnet was lifted, for the car's engine had been modified to meet the American emission requirements. These changes were introduced progressively and, in the first instance, applied only to crankcase breathing. But more elaborate modifications followed. The work was undertaken by Howard Dancocks and Harry Dewick at the BMC research centre based at the Longbridge East Works. The most obvious new component was an engine-driven injection pump that squirted air into the exhaust ports so that any unburnt gases, that had survived that far, completed the combustion process. Also incorporated was a relief valve to limit the pump's output at

that the MGB's twin SU carburettors were unable to meet the emission demands. Therefore, from 1975, they were dispensed with on cars sold in the United States and replaced by a single Stromberg Zenith unit. Not surprisingly, performance suffered in the process.

Inside, the 1968 American cars were fitted with a special dashboard laid out by Jim O'Neill. This had a new recessed instrument panel while the passenger's side of the facia was completely altered. The glove

The Mark 11 MGB GT for 1968, externally identical to its predecessors. Such changes as did occur were below the surface, the principal alteration being the introduction of a wider gearbox tunnel to accept a new, all-synchromesh gearbox, as demanded for the simultaneously introduced six cylinder MGC.

high revs along with a non-return valve to prevent the blow back of exhaust gases. The outlet side of the pump was connected to the inlet manifold, via an appropriately named gulp valve, to consume any neat petrol remaining after a prolonged period of high speed running. Less obviously, but none the less important, was a special petrol tank with a separate fuel separation sector, sealed filler cap, associated pipery and under bonnet canister. But as the legislation became increasingly severe, it was found

compartment was dispensed with and replaced by a padded surround that Roy Brocklehurst called the Abingdon Pillow. The results were rather severe and later the dash was modified and the glove box reintroduced, for 1972.

The extraordinary amount of work necessary to modify US specification Bs for the January 1968 start date resulted in MGB production falling back badly in 1967. Roadster production totalled 14,568 and 11,067 GTs were built. In addition Abingdon

The American safety regulations came into force on 1 January 1968. This was one of the first experimental dashboards, photographed early in 1967, with the ugly,

energy-absorbing 'Abingdon pillow' which was fortunately modified over the years. A head restraint and safety steering wheel was also featured.

The finished product, the dashboard being peculiar to the American cars. The heater control is on the left of the steering column, and the rectangular instrument between the rev counter and speedometer is the oil pressure gauge. The steering column stalks are also new and, at this stage, only applied to the American specification cars. The left-hand one was responsible for dipping, flashing and indicating, while pushing the end of the right-hand one activated the windscreen wipers and moving the lever backwards and forwards operated the overdrive which was an improvement on the original arrangement. Restructuring the dashboard necessitated repositioning the radio in the central console which, in turn, meant that the loudspeaker was positioned in the door. The rocker switches would not appear on British MGBs until 1972. The presence of the new all-synchromesh gearbox is indicated by the short gear lever with its round, rather than elongated, gear knob.

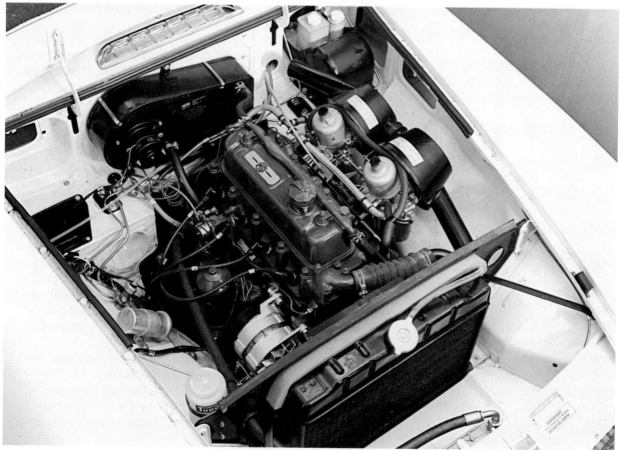

The engine compartment of the American specification MGB for 1968. The most obvious modification is the engine-driven air injection pump, with the Cooper air cleaner directly below. The air injection manifold is located directly above the sparking plugs. This new equipment represented the first stage of under-bonnet modifications on those cars destined for the US market.

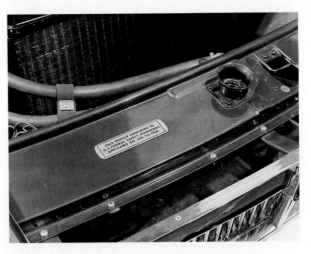

The indication that the 1968 MGBs, destined for the United States, conformed to the all-important American safety regulations. December 1967 'was the only time I've ever worked through Christmas!' recalls Don Hayter.

was also wrestling with the problems of putting the MGC into production; and the tribulations of that particular exercise are set down in Chapter Three. This six-cylinder version of the MGB was launched at the 1967 Motor Show and the B also benefited from its all-synchromesh gearbox and wider transmission tunnel. This permitted the introduction of an automatic MGB, clearly aimed at the American market, which continued as an option until 1973.

If 1968 was important to Abingdon in that it saw the introduction of special MGBs for the American market, then there were more corporate upheavals for BMC (now British Motor Holdings) following a merger with Jaguar in 1966. Sir Leonard Lord had been suffering from ill health for some years when he handed over the running of the Corporation's affairs to George Harriman (knighted in 1965) in 1961. At this juncture, BMC's fortunes appeared outwardly buoyant. It had launched its sensational front wheel drive Mini in 1959 and had followed it up with a 1100 derivative which, in 1965, contributed to the Corporation's massive 38 per cent of new car sales. It was Harriman and Alec Issigonis, the latter having been made BMC's technical director in 1961 and board member two years later, who were to steer BMC through the treacherous waters of the nineteen sixties.

There were also under-bonnet changes on the non-US specification cars for the 1968 model year. The most obvious modification was the introduction of a Lucas 16AC alternator, which replaced the dynamo hitherto employed, and which meant that the electrical system was now negative earth rather than positive. Note the new vertically mounted oil filter though the new pre-engaged starter motor, which dispensed with the Bendix spring previously fitted, cannot be seen. As a result of all these changes, the engine was redesignated Type 18 GD.

Issigonis, whose genius had created the Mini, and who readily admitted his preference for small car design, was convinced that within a decade front wheel drive would be the order of the day. The theory was that BMC should produce technically advanced designs, which would enjoy long production runs, so the heavy tooling costs required to develop new models could, accordingly, be reduced. Ford, BMC's chief rivals in the motoring market place, by contrast, opted for conventional engineering with regular model changes.

Its Cortina which, like the MGB, was launched at the 1962 Motor Show, exemplified this alternative design philosophy and soon began to eat into BMC sales. By 1966 the Corporation's market share had dropped to 34 per cent, also partly due to the failure of the new 1800 model to find its form. In 1967 their market share fell again and, in 1968, the Cortina briefly overtook the Austin/Morris 1100 as Britain's top-selling car. The combine had made itself ripe for take-over and it came in the shape of Sir Donald Stokes and Leyland Motors. Leyland, commercial vehicle manufacturers since 1897, had in the post-war years been keen to diversify into the car market. In 1961 it had taken over the ailing Standard-Triumph company and snapped up Rover in 1967. After prolonged behind the scenes negotiations, in January 1968 a merger between British Motor Holdings and Leyland was announced and ratified in May. Although Sir George Harri-

MGB
The illustrated history

man was given the position of chairman he stepped down eight months later; Sir Donald Stokes, the driving force of the new British Leyland Motor Corporation, took over the corporate reins completely at the end of 1968.

For MG, unlike BMC, the sixties had represented a period of progressive, unparalleled growth. But the Leyland hierarchy was dominated by former Triumph executives who had produced the rival range of TR sports cars which MG had consistently outsold in the fifties and sixties. John Thornley is convinced that MG's fate was sealed from that time and it is difficult to argue with this contention. Today, this view is confirmed by John Barber, British Leyland's managing director and deputy chairman who was finance director during the corporation's formative years. He recalls, 'There was often conflict between Triumph and MG. Donald Stokes and George Turnbull [managing director of the Austin Morris division] were Triumph people and they were quite ruthless about it: Triumph was going to have the sports car market – I think it was completely the wrong decision'. Leyland attitude to Abingdon is perhaps underlined by MG being lumped in with the Austin Morris manufacturing group where it should logically have been part of the Specialist Car division which consisted of Jaguar, Rover *and* Triumph.

Nineteen sixty-nine saw John Thornley's retirement through ill health as MG's general manager, his place being taken by Leslie (Les) Lambourne, who went to Abingdon in 1958 and had been assistant general manager since 1967. John Thornley had presided over the most successful period of MG's history during his 17 years at its head. During his stewardship the MG factory became the world's largest producer of sports cars and the MGA's record output was subsequently surpassed by the MGB. He chose his subordinates with great care which was an undoubted factor in nurturing the indefinable 'Abingdon touch' which reached back to the firm's pre-war days.

Soon after the creation of British Ley-

land, the new management began thinking in terms of producing a corporate sports car intended to replace the TR6 and the MGB. At Canley, now operating under Spen King's direction, Triumph opted for a conventional front-engined design but Abingdon went in for a far more ambitious package. Colin Chapman had already produced the Lotus Europa, the world's first series production mid-engined sports car in 1966. It was an exciting theme and MG decided that the MGD, as it would have been, should follow this configuration. The design was coded ADO 21 and its project office was opened at Abingdon on 11 November 1969. John Thornley, it should be added, had been fiercely anti-mid-engine. 'I entirely agree that it is the correct configuration for a maximum performance vehicle but how does one sell a car in quantity if one puts the engine where the children ought to be?'

Don Hayter, who had taken over the MG projects department in 1968, was responsible for the new car's layout and he undertook the work at Longbridge with the body conceived alongside the mechanics. ADO 21's underframe and suspension were completely new but the engine and its attendant transmission was the four-cylinder 1750cc E Series Maxi unit while the 2.2 litre six-cylinder version was an alternative fitment. The Maxi engine/transmission was mounted centrally, and transversely, behind the driving compartment. Although the radiator was attached to the engine there were also thoughts about mounting it at the front of the car (the surviving drawings show both locations) with the intention of improving weight distribution. Suspension was by struts front and rear with two rear suspension layouts considered. The first, which was fitted to a specially converted MGB GT with a fabricated bulkhead and no tailgate, employed a de Dion tube, mounted *ahead* of the differential which pushed the car along on a large universal joint. A Watts linkage was also incorporated. The alternative system, parts of which were made but never fitted to a vehicle, used the de Dion in the conventional position, multiple leaf springs and no Watts linkage. The modified GT was fitted with the E4 1750cc engine and sat on 13 inch wheels which were thus smaller than the MGB ones. Don Hayter recalls that the layout came up to expectations though there were the inevitable minor problems with throttle linkages.

Yet another MG that might have been, the mid-engined ADO 21, photographed at Longbridge in November 1970, though the car's mechanical layout was undertaken at Abingdon. In an in-house competition between MG and Triumph, the latter won and the outcome was the TR7 of 1975, effectively a front-engined version of this styling exercise by Harris Mann. But the TR7's arrival spelled death, in the long term, for the ageing MGB and its Abingdon factory.

ADO 21 was styled at Longbridge by Harris Mann, who had joined Leyland from Ford. The MGD was sensational, a true wedge shape, 4164mm long, 1730mm wide and 1160mm high, made possible by the mid-engined location. A wood and clay mock-up was produced at the Longbridge styling studio to await viewing by the British Leyland management in November 1970. When it came to a choice between it and Triumph's front engined Bullet project it came down in favour of the car from Canley. But, ironically, the resulting TR7 was, in every sense, a compromise between the two projects. Although ADO 21's styling was much admired, and it was decided that the new Triumph sports car should embody the MGD's wedge, the Triumph Bullet was *front*-engined and its location meant a dilution of the ADO 21 proportions; the results were controversial to say the least. The resulting Triumph TR7 coupé was launched on the American market at the beginning of 1975, the MGB GT having been withdrawn in the United States to make way for it. If the TR7's looks were against it there was also a

stream of trans-Atlantic complaints about the new TR's quality. Clearly the Triumph plant at Speke, Liverpool was no Abingdon. Production reached MGB-like proportions for one year only when, in 1976, 27, 657 TR7s were built with output falling back to 12,106 in 1977. An open version (which was initially to have been MG badged), a great visual improvement over the closed car, appeared in 1980 but after moving from Speke to Canley and finally to Solihull, the TR7 finally ceased production in October 1981 after 111,648 had been built. This six-year-old model out-produced the 18-year-old MGB by just twelve months.

But, for MG, the cancellation of ADO 21 meant that it lacked a sports car to take it into the 1980s. Roy Brocklehurst puts the axeing of the MGD into perspective: 'I wouldn't be arrogant enough to say that the Leyland management took the wrong decision when ADO 21 was cancelled. I wouldn't argue with the decision, we didn't at the time. Ours was an advanced vehicle and, apart from the engine/gearbox unit, it was completely new from stem to stern and would have required an enormous investment to produce. But it was *our* decision to go mid-engined. We sealed our own fate but we couldn't have known it at the time.'

Another design concept that also dates from the same period as ADO 21 was the Condor project. This car was not intended to replace the MGB but, as a four-seater coupé, would have been an additional model. It was the nearest that British Leyland got to producing an equivalent to Ford's newly introduced Capri and would have been fitted with a variety of engines, including the

E4 and E6 Maxi units and the Rover V8. The idea, which dated from November 1968, was coded EX 242 in the MG design register and ADO 68 in corporate language. It was based on the floor pan of ADO 28, destined to emerge as the Morris Marina in 1971. In the latter days of BMC, Roy Haynes had joined the corporation from Ford as director of styling. Haynes had been responsible for the Marina's styling and he also has the Con-

The first major facelift on the MGB came on the 1970 model year cars, and followed MG's becoming part of the Austin Morris division of the British Leyland Motor Corporation. This recessed radiator grille, with its chrome surround and new MG badge contained within two lines of octagons, thankfully only endured until 1972. It was not designed at Abingdon but

dor's lines to his credit. There was also an alternative convertible version, which was MG badged and, like ADO 21, a clay mock-up was produced at Longbridge. But the project was stillborn and Condor became another MG might-have-been.

Despite these upheavals, MGB production continued to rise. Output stood at 31,030 in 1969, went up again to 36,570 in 1970 and, despite a dip to 34,68 in 1971, bounced back in 1972 with a record 39,393 MGBs produced.

at British Leyland's Longbridge head quarters and was inflicted on MG even though it left the bonnet moulding, indicating the original position of the MG badge, looking out of place. This is the American specification car with rubber overrider inserts, which were not fitted to the right-hand drive cars until 1971, and triple windscreen wipers which were only fitted to the open cars.

Syd Enever retired in March 1971, having reached his sixty-fifth birthday, and was replaced by Roy Brocklehurst. Syd had latterly become disillusioned by the dilution of the MG persona that had been taking place under the BMC and, later, British Leyland regimes. In the late 1960s, with retirement on the horizon, when he confided to his friend and colleague David Ash, he was probably speaking for many of his

contemporaries: 'It won't change. At least not in my time. There is no money for anything new. We have simply got to make do and hope for the best. There is no other way.' Ash believes that Enever is 'that rare kind of genius who had a special gift for quantum. Cars such as the TD, TF, MGA and MGB and his variegated assortment of land speed record cars came off his drawing board with a rightness and perfection, not just of line and style, but balance and practicality that were his hallmark . . . Like

most men of this unusual stripe, I found Enever always frank, almost blunt even, and utterly unpretentious. In his years at MG there was never any posturing. While many others deferred to him constantly, Syd Enever seemed always to see himself as a very mortal, even ordinary human being – although automotive history will record that he was vastly more important and gifted than that.'

113

Rear of the American specification car,
showing the split bumper, with number
plate lights contained within the open
sections, which was only employed for a
year. The MG logo was coloured.

The works hardtop was still available in
1969 with the glass rear window affording
excellent visibility.

An American specification car with the
hood lowered, revealing the head rests.
The MGB roadster sold for $2817 in
America in 1970.

Driving compartment of the 1970 US specification car, with new, smaller leather-covered steering wheel. This was fitted across the MGB range as were the new, reclining seats which were Vinyl covered, so usurping leather upholstery after seven years. The headrests were fitted as standard equipment only on these American cars for one year. The choke control over the water temperature gauge has acquired a T-shaped lever.

Opposite Top: The complete 1970 American MG range with Midgets, also fitted with side-mounted reflectors, in the foreground and the entire MGB left-hand drive family in the background.   *Far Left:* A GT, all set for the American market. Note the small British Leyland Motor Corporation badges fixed on the front wings just ahead of the doors, which were fitted on both sides of the car from the 1970 models and featured on all MGBs until 1976.   *Left:* A 1970 model year right-hand drive B. Note that the rubber overrider inserts have not been extended to these British cars. The price was £1125.   *Above:* The 1970 right-hand drive roadster, displaying the new seats and door trim and the distinctive three-spoked steering wheel. The indicator stalk on the right of the steering column has been replaced by a new unit which also operates the dip switch, so dispensing with the floor-mounted unit, and the horn.   *Below:* A line-up of American specification GTs. They show that wire wheels were still available as optional extras but highlight how the new recessed radiator grille completely unsettled the visual appearance of the front of the MGB, giving it a bulbous, over-heavy appearance.

MGB
The illustrated history

The right-hand drive cars were fitted with new rear lenses for 1970. The *BGT* badge was also new and, like the new radiator grille, also came from British Leyland and replaced the lettering each side of the octagon.

Automatic transmission on a 1970 MGB, which was introduced in 1968, and remained available until 1973. Although a standard three-speed Type 35 Borg-Warner unit, the selector mechanism was peculiar to MG and was the work of the redoubtable Syd Enever. The lever itself moved through a notched gate which was marked, P, R, N, D, L2, L1 respectively though a 'cotton reel' on the lever had to be lifted to clear the safety stop between the reverse and neutral. Engaging L1 held the transmission in first gear, regardless of engine revs. When L2 was engaged it provided a positive hold on intermediate ratios, without excluding bottom gear. From starting, this meant that the car remained in its intermediate range, up to about 80 mph, after which the D slot was engaged. With this layout the gearchange was made to resemble more closely that of a conventional gearbox. The small map reading light, which was used to illuminate the controls at night, can also be seen. Note the new door trims, introduced simultaneously with the reclining seats. (Courtesy Motor)

A 1971 roadster on the move, a year in which overriders with rubber inserts, introduced on the American specifications car from 1968, were extended to the right-hand drive cars.

The driving compartment of the 1971 roadster, looking much as it did in 1970 with the exception of the fully-gaitered gear lever. Beneath the bonnet was an uprated heater with revised ducting inside the car.

In the meantime, Don Hayter was up to his eyes in the ramifications of the American safety legislation as all British Leyland's air bag and other safety work had been transferred to Abingdon. Then there were the MGB's bumpers that had to be redesigned for the American market. The first renderings were known at Abingdon as 'Sabrina bumpers' having somewhat ample overriders and being fitted to American sold Bs from 1974. Don was also responsible for the creation of a one-off MGB (EX 250) of 1972 which embodied current and future safety ideas for exhibition in Washington. This car still survives as part of the British Motor Industry's Trust's Collection.

The safety modification that was completely to alter the appearance of the MGB from the 1975 model year was the fitment of massive polyurethane bumpers which, for production reasons, had to be fitted to cars produced for the home market as well as the American one. The styling of the bumpers was dictated by Longbridge, and Jim O'Neill first went ahead and designed one in conjunction with the Cable Belt Company but the rubber units that resulted proved unpredictable and difficult to produce. So another material was tried. 'We knew we could mould in polyurethane but we didn't know how good a finish we could get,' recalls Hayter, 'so we got in touch with Marley Foam of Lenham, Kent, and Jim O'Neill took out a patent, on Leyland's behalf, for a progressive deformation process and they eventually produced them for us.' But their fitment did upset the MGBs looks, something that Don Hayter, who had styled the car back in 1958, readily admits. Also the new bumpers considerably added to the car's weight and thus detracted from its performance. The original chrome ones

The 250,000th MGB was built in May 1971, which prompted a visit from George Turnbull, managing director of the Austin Morris Division of British Leyland of which MG was a part. The car, an American specification GT, was subsequently photographed with 'Old Number One'. The MG development department is shown here with Alec Hounslow, chief development engineer, in a suit in the centre of the picture.

Changes in the 1972 model year were confined to the car's interior. The most obvious difference was the introduction of face level adjustable air vents, which were located where the radio had previously been housed. Also rocker switches, a feature of the American specifications cars since 1968, also appeared. There was a new, central console to contain the radio, when fitted, and the interior light can be seen through the spokes of the steering wheel, which remained unchanged. The arm rest between the seats is hinged and there was storage space beneath. Brushed nylon seats were also introduced from the autumn of 1971.

A storm of protest, particularly from America, to the recessed radiator intake resulted in British Leyland's giving the MGB its grille back for 1973 and, although it used cheaper mesh rather than chrome slats, it was an enormous improvement. The *BGT* badge at the rear was changed to a smaller rendering at the same time. A heated rear window was standardised.

Right: The 1973 roadster, also looking all the better for its new grille. Matt black windscreen wipers also replaced the chrome-plated ones hitherto fitted. A tonneau cover became a standard fitting.

More interior changes for 1973. There was a new, light alloy leather-covered slotted-spoke steering wheel with a matching gear lever knob. A cigar lighter, located on the console, became a standard fitment. The GT seats were fitted with these full-width nylon coverings, while the roadster used a mixture of vinyl and nylon. Padded arm rests were also introduced in both doors.

had weighed just 33 lb but by the time the production MGB had been fitted with the new design, the modifications and units themselves added 105 lb, or close on a hundredweight, to the car. Things were made worse by the fact that the MGB had to be raised so the bumper height would conform to the American requirement that they should be 16 to 20 inches above the ground. Not only did this upset the car's proportions but it also introduced an unacceptable element of body roll, only resolved to some extent by the fitting of a rear anti-roll bar from 1976. The front one was thickened

up at the same time. This radical modification to the MGB's specification saw it allocated ADO 76 as its new corporate number.

The problems in achieving American emission standards were to dominate the MGB's latter years, a little known side effect of which was the creation of Leyland's new O Series engine that replaced the B Series unit and first appeared on the revised Princess range in mid-1978. The new unit was created largely because the rigorous emission laws demanded that engines be capable of sustaining specified emission minima for a

This Anniversary model appeared in 1975 and was limited to the GT. Distinctive features are the V8 type wheels and British Racing Green and gold livery.

A contemporary publicity photograph, shot at Palace House, Beaulieu. The car is a 1975 model year GT, when the polyurethane bumpers were introduced. They are just discernible in this picture though the extra ride height, note the gap between the top of the wheel and the arch, is more obvious. The car in the foreground is the National Motor Museum's Alfonso Hispano-Suiza with a 1935 MG in the background.

distance of 50,000 miles although routine maintenance was allowable within this span. On the B Series engine, the design of which went back to the early post-war years, its Achilles' heel was the squew gear used to drive the distributor from the side-mounted camshaft. The gear would wear, allowing the spark timing to wander and the engine to go off tune; the exhaust emissions would deteriorate in the process.

Many attempts were made to circumvent the problem but, eventually, the British Leyland management decided that the only answer was to design a completely new engine for the MGB, because it was the company's largest American seller. The engine would also be used, of course, for other models within the corporate fold. But there was another snag in that new machinery had been recently installed at Long-

A batch of foreshortened MGBs pictured at Abingdon after they had been crash tested to evaluate them for the all important American market. (Courtesy John Seager)

The most radical change in the appearance of the British specification MGB came in the 1975 model year, with the arrival of these energy-absorbing bumpers. Made by Marley Foam from Bayflex 90 polyurethane, they were fitted front and rear as demanded by the American safety regulations. They were required not to deform in the event of a 5 mph impact and concealed substantial reinforcing beams.

On the debit side the MGB lost its traditional radiator grille, added 70 lb to its weight, which went up to 20.4 cwt in roadster form, and added a further five inches to its length. In addition, to conform to the American regulations, the ride height also had to be increased by 1.5 inches, achieved by packing the front suspension and increasing the camber of the rear springs, which tended to upset the car's handling. The D type overdrive was replaced by the LH unit.

There were 750 examples made of this 1975 limited edition 'Jubilee' GT model, which cost £2669 instead of the usual £2539 for the standard model. Finished in British Racing Green with gold side stripes, it was fitted with tinted windows, head restraints, overdrive and these handsome alloy V8 wheels, which took wider, 175 section tyres. The transfers on the side of the front wings read *MG 1925–1975*, suggesting that the car was celebrating the 50th anniversary of the marque, whereas, the first MG had actually appeared in 1924! British Leyland responded by claiming that the car was commemorating the 50th anniversary of Cecil Kimber's first class award in the 1925 Lands End Trial in 'Old Number One'.

bridge for the manufacture of the B Series crankshaft, so the new power unit, designed under Geoffrey Johnson's direction, had to be founded on this item. Prototype O Series engines used B Series crankshafts, but the nose was subsequently lengthened.

Above: The 1975 GT was similarly disfigured and, further to the additions on the roadster, automatic seat belts became a standard fitment.

Below: The engine of the Waters car. Note the belt driven air injection pump and single Stromberg carburettor, fitted to the American specification cars from the 1975 model year.

Left: This 1977 American specification roadster never crossed the Atlantic but spent all its life in Britain. Owned by Danny Waters, it still retains all its special equipment even down to its sealed beam headlamps instead of the usual halogen units.

The rapidly ageing MG range for 1976, with the MGB roadster and GT in the foreground and the Midget, with which it shared Rostyle wheels from 1972 and was also fitted with energy absorbing bumpers, in the background. The MGB GT V8 ceased production in July of 1976.

Interior of the US spec. car. By this time UK and US car again shared essentially the same styling.

The 1977 roadster, with quartz halogen headlamps, introduced that year. They were also fitted to the GT which was offered with tinted windows as standard. Both models benefited from thicker anti-roll bars front and rear to counter the effects of the increased ride height.

In September 1979, BL Cars organised a gathering at Abingdon to commemorate the 50th anniversary of the MG's move to the town. The parade included this Berlinette 1800, by Jacques Coune, followed by EX 234, and a string of MGCs.

EX 234 pictured during the 1979 celebrations, owned by MG enthusiast Syd Beer. Note its registration number, which echoed the initials of R.E. Ward, one time MG plant director. However, on 10 September, forever known within MG circles as Black Monday, BL announced that MGB production would cease and the Abingdon factory close.

News of the end of the MGB and the proposed closure of the Abingdon factory produced an instantaneous response from the MG Owners' Club and the MG Car Club. This culminated in a demonstration held in London, on Sunday 30 September 1979, a mere 20 days after Black Monday. Here the march assembles in London's Arundel Street, with Temple underground station in the background, prior to gathering at the Aldwych starting point.

From there the calvalcade of MGs of all ages proceeded to Trafalgar Square and then to Piccadilly where it halted outside Nuffield House, on the left. Note the BL Cars badge, and office of chairman, Sir Michael Edwardes. There a petition was handed in which protested against news of the proposed Abingdon closure and the marque's doubtful future.

MGB
The illustrated history

Once experimental engines were produced, they were fitted to MGBs in 1972/3, and Abingdon embarked on a series of test programmes. The oversquare 84 x 75mm 1695cc four was an overhead camshaft unit with its distributor prominent and accessible at right angles to the shaft. But, tragically, this engine, conceived with the MGB in mind, was never fitted to the model which soldiered on with the ageing B Series unit. The reasons for this decision have never been made public but it seems likely that, by the time the O Series engine was ready for production, the MGB was nearing the end of its manufacturing life. The fact that it was fitted with the B engine, which the O progressively made obsolete, meant that by 1979 there were no other Leyland cars fitted with it which gave the then BL management a reason to axe the car.

These developments are to anticipate our story somewhat because there were more changes at MG in 1973. In July, Roy Brocklehurst left Abingdon to become chief engineer, Vehicle Engineering for Austin Morris at Longbridge. His place at MG was taken by Don Hayter. By this time work had been completed on the Rover engined MGB GT V8 which went into production in 1973, and continued to be built until 1976, details of which are set down in the next Chapter. Incredibly, MGB production continued to hold up, though in 1973/4 output at around the 29,000 mark was 10,000 below the 1972 peak. Output dipped badly to 24,576 in 1975 but perked up again to 29,558 in the following year.

In 1974 it had been planned to celebrate MG's 50th anniversary with a special edition of the car, but the launch was put off until 1975. Maybe, it was the 50th anniversary of Cecil Kimber's 'Old Number One' special built in 1925. This 'Anniversary' model was limited to 750 GTs, finished in British Racing Green with gold striping. The special aluminium wheels of the V8 model were standardised as was tinted glass, head restraints and overdrive.

By the mid-seventies, Leyland, MGs parent to whom it looked for the reinvest-

ment for new models, was in deep trouble. In 1971 its market share had stood at a healthy 40.2 per cent, but this continued to drop every subsequent year in the face of inroads from the sure-footed professionalism of Ford and from foreign imports. This culminated in an acute cash flow problem at the end of 1974, the energy crisis triggered by the Arab/Israeli war of 1973 having produced the knock-out blow. In 1975 came the controversial Ryder Report and, in July,

The export compound at Abingdon pictured in 1978 with the then current polyurethane bumpered GT in the foreground, flanked on the right by a chrome bumpered roadster, its MGA predecessor on the left with MGC GT and current roadster behind. (Courtesy Piers J.S. Hubbard.)

Left: For 1977 the MGB received its first radical facia facelift since 1962 even though the glove compartment remained! The speedometer and rev counter were carried over from the 1975 cars though the original shroud was discontinued and the heater received a two-speed fan. The improved central console was fitted with a different interior light and an electric clock, while the long-criticised heater knobs were replaced by more efficient controls located each side of it. The overdrive switch was moved from the left-hand stalk, Triumph manner, to the gear lever knob. Seats were finished in this smart, striped trim, a theme that was perpetuated in the standardised headrests. The lower-geared four-spoke steering wheel was also new, while the pedal positions were also changed to permit, at long last, heel and toeing. From April 1977, the roadster was fitted with inertia reel seat belts as standard.

British Leyland was nationalised. Chairmen came and went but it wasn't until November 1977 that Michael Edwardes took over as chairman at a time when Leyland Cars' market share had slumped to 24 per cent. Edwardes inherited a combine that was producing too few cars from too many plants – there were 29 in all – and where there had been reinvestment, the resulting models often lacked public appeal. The first casualty was the Triumph TR7 factory at Speke, Liverpool, which was closed in May 1978. Edwardes renamed the business BL Cars and revived marque names so that MG, instead of being 'Leyland Assembly Plant, Abingdon', once more became 'MG Cars, Abingdon' – but not, alas, for long.

By the summer of 1979, BL Cars' problem of deteriorating finances was further exacerbated by the rising value of the pound; a trend that had started at the beginning of 1979 and accelerated with the Conservative election victory in May. The situation became so serious that, in July, Edwardes and his top management team met at Ye Olde Bell, Hurley, Berkshire to try to resolve the problem. An outcome of this meeting was the decision that the BL workforce would have to be cut by a further 25,000. The Triumph factory at Canley would have to close while MG production at Abingdon would also have to cease and with it the MGB. Such was the high value of the pound against the dollar that, in the summer of 1979, BL calculated it was losing £900 on every MGB it sold in America.

The decision was made public on 10 September 1979, which coincided with a visit of American dealers to Abingdon to celebrate the 50th anniversary of the company's move there; the date has since gone down in MG history as Black Monday. Such was the public outcry, and the measure of the high standing that the MG name still enjoyed, that Edwardes subsequently wrote in *Back from the Brink* (Collins, 1983): 'The decision to stop MG sports car production created more public fuss and misunderstanding than anything in the whole five years – even greater than wholesale factory closures and massive job losses.'

John Thornley, who had worked for MG for 33 years recalls his memories of that fateful day: 'The news kicked the MG hive and there was a great deal of buzzing, but I had an uneasy feeling that this wouldn't get us anywhere. Maybe I had a better idea than

most of the strength of the opposition. My first thoughts were, of course, for all those with whom I had worked all those years, but I couldn't see what to do. I stuck my hands deep in my pockets and walked around for all of a couple of days with my eyes on the ground. The answer came quite suddenly.

'In the months immediately preceding, BL had withdrawn from the US market the Sprite, the Midget and the Spitfire. If the MGB now ceased as well, it would spell bankruptcy for many of the dealers. And they were my friends. So I decided to write to warn them and tried to get them to act collectively to get the decision reversed.'

He decided to talk to Syd Beer of Houghton, Cambridgeshire, a great MG enthusiast and collector. John explained his scheme and, having penned a letter, Beer arranged for it to be duplicated. In the meantime, a list of MG dealers had been obtained from BL. Significantly, the most up to date one available dated back to 1974. John was collected from Abingdon in that fateful September and, at Sydney Beer's house, he signed 450 letters which were then packaged in envelopes that had already been addressed to MG's American dealers. Fortunately there was a US airbase near the Beer residence, where Syd had bought 450 15 cent American stamps, which were duly stuck on the pre-addressed envelopes. Then, Thornley's letters were transported, somewhat unofficially, to the United States, by courtesy of the US Air Force. On arrival they were posted, so within a week of the BL announcement, MG's trans-Atlantic retailers were informed of the state of affairs at Abingdon. 'The letter basically said, "this is going to ruin you unless you can get this decision changed." I felt that this was the only way, if there was one, of reversing the intended closure,' recalls Thornley.

Although there was an American outcry, the protests were, alas, all in vain. But there was one further attempt to save the MGB, and Abingdon, before the blow finally fell. In October 1979, just a month after the BL's bombshell, came news of a plan for a consortium, led by Alan Curtis of Aston Martin, who had put together a £30 million pound package to rescue MG. There followed months of negotiations with Leyland and Sir Michael Edwardes and, on 1 April 1980, it was announced that the consortium had reached agreement with the corporation that the MGB and Abingdon

500,000TH MGB

The half millionth MGB was built in January 1980. Syd Enever, left, then 73, returned to the factory for this historic photograph, Don Hayter, chief engineer, on his left with Terry Mitchell, chief chassis designer and Jim O'Neill, chief body designer, on the other side of the car. (Courtesy Don Hayter)

What would have been the 1981 model year MGB, if there had been one, distinguished by these new alloy wheels. In June 1980, rear fog lamps had been standardised. The price was £6127, with the GT costing £6595.

were to continue. The two parties issued a joint statement which read: 'The consortium will buy MG's Abingdon plant in Oxfordshire, together with the worldwide exclusive licence for the building and sale of MG cars.' It was not to be, however, for an arctic economic climate prevented Curtis from raising sufficient funds and, on 1 July 1980, BL announced that the MGB was to cease production and the Abingdon factory close.

In early 1981 BL was to announce the Limited Edition – 'a rare and final edition of the most loved, famous sports car that has ever been built'. These were the last 1000 MGBs, less the final two, off the production line, finished in pewter or bronze metallic paint, and available with alloy or wire wheels. The Abingdon

MGB
The illustrated history

workforce was run down and, on Wednesday 22 October, 1980, just over a year after the Black Monday announcement, the last two MGBs were completed.

John Thornley, having met up with Syd Enever and historian F. Wilson McComb, who had so enthusiastically edited the MG Car Club's own *Safety First* magazine from 1959 until 1964, drove to the old factory to witness the occasion where they were joined by chief engineer Don Hayter and MG plant manager Chris Peacock. There were the last two Limited Edition MGBs, a bronze tourer, chassis number G-HN5 523001, and the final car, a pewter GT (G-HD5 523002).

This 1980 GT is owned by Brian Holland.

Interior of the 1980 GT.

. . . and is an MG Car Club concours winner.

End of the line. The LE (Limited Edition) MGBs fitted with front spoilers and the choice of alloy or wire wheels. The roadster was finished in bronze metallic paint and there was LE side livery running the length of the bodywork. The interior was in orange and brown and the car sold for £6445. The GT, in a pewter metallic hue, with silver livery had a silver/grey interior. The price was £6937. The last two cars, a roadster chassis number 523,001 and GT 523002, were retained by BL for its collection of historic vehicles. The last American specification car was presented to Henry Ford 11 for exhibition at the Henry Ford Museum, Dearborn, USA.

What might have been. On 18 October 1980, five weeks after Black Monday, news broke that a consortium, lead by Alan Curtis of Aston Martin, had been formed in the hope of saving the MGB and its Abingdon factory. William Towns was responsible for designing what would have been the 1981 MGB. Built at Aston Martin's Newport Pagnell factory, this car featured a GT windscreen and doors, and Towns managed to squeeze in a miniature MGB grille just above the 'rubber' bumpers, while a second steel skin, finished in contrasting black, was attached to the lower portion of the body which was no doubt intended to lessen the visual impact of the bumpers. The alloy wheels were also new.

A rear view of the same car with new rear light treatment. Although, on 1 April 1980 it was announced that the consortium had reached agreement with BL to produce the MGB under licence at Abingdon, the rapidly deteriorating financial climate, in the wake of the 1979 oil price rise, wrought havoc with these plans and a last minute approach to the Japanese Toyota company in July 1980 to take a majority shareholding in the consortium, came too late.

MGB
The illustrated history

It was to be another day before the workforce of A Block, which was the main assembly plant, finally left Abingdon on 24 October though those employed in B Block, which concerned itself with final vehicle rectification, didn't depart until the end of the following week, on 31 October. Chief engineer Don Hayter, manager Chris Peacock and administrative staff stayed on for a further six weeks, finally leaving on 12 December 1980. Hayter recalls: 'the board room was getting emptier and emptier. In the end there was just production and plant engineering manager Doug Gardner, Norman Higgins of finance and myself'

From thereon Doug Gardner remained in charge of the empty factory, and auction sales of plant and office equipment were held on 18/20/23 and 24th March 1981. At 2 pm on 21 April the MG factory became the property of the Standard Life Assurance Company though it wasn't until 13 June that BL Motor Sport, as the MG Special Tuning department had become, transferred to Cowley. Gardner continued on the premises until Friday 3 July when he and Mrs Sheila Godwin, who had undertaken secretarial duties, left the MG works for the last time.

The small building which had housed an electrical sub station on A Block also survives. The MG telephone exchange was on its first floor and its number (Abingdon 251) was used, in 0251 form, as the prefix for MG chassis numbers prior to the arrival of the TF model in 1953.

The entrance to the MG factory. This is Gate 3 on the Marcham Road which was demolished to make way for the Abingdon Business Park. (Courtesy John Seager)

Happier days! This notice, attached to the wall of A block, facing the Marcham Road, proclaimed this all important message. The motif in the bottom left-hand corner is that of the firm's Leyland Cars' parent. (Courtesy John Seager)

Another survivor is the former MG office block in Cemetery Road, which has been refurbished and taken over by the Abingdon Business Park. Cecil Kimber's office, and the one occupied by John Thornley from 1956 to 1969, was the far room on the first floor, with a bay window which overlooked the MG plant.

The LE (for Limited Edition) MGB, although built in 1980 did not go on sale until January of the following year and after the Abingdon factory had ceased production. This example is fitted with optional alloy wheels with 185/70 tyres, which were £359 extra, and is owned by Geoff Simpson.

End of the line. The last MGB body to be built by Pressed Steel at its factory at Stratton St Margaret, near Swindon. The date is 2 October 1980.

This is how it arrived at Abingdon, decked with bunting and union jacks. (Courtesy John Seager)

VYC 198W

Left: Abingdon 1980, the last year of the MGB's production. Here a body is being lowered from the upper trim deck to the production line proper. (Courtesy John Seager)

Bottom left: The GT assembly at Abingdon after the engine/gearbox unit and suspension have been fitted. (Courtesy John Seager)

Top: This magnificent styling exercise, MG EX-E, the work of Austin Rover's styling director Roy Axe, made a surprise appearance at the 1985 Frankfurt Motor Show, to universal acclaim. It was also a public demonstration of the company's commitment to the MG name. Thus MG has outlived its Morris parent, that ceased as a marque name in 1983, and will also outstrip the Austin one, which also seems destined to disappear.

Above: The MG name was in abeyance from October 1980 until May 1982, when it reappeared on the best-selling version of the 1.3 litre Metro, an appropriately sporting hatchback, with a top line 93bhp Turbo model arriving for 1983. Since then the MG name has been extended to performance versions of the Maestro and Montego models and now appears to have a secure future. This is a 1988 car.

This is the last MGB (G-HN5 521996) to be exported, a Porcelain White roadster destined for Japan. The notice on its windscreen reads 'The Last One?' It was not . . . (Courtesy John Seager)

. . . but this was. The date is Thursday 23 October 1980 and the GT (G-HD5 523002) on the right is. It is pictured at the factory with the two individuals most responsible for the MGB's creation: John Thornley, left, with his GT with its famous MG 1 number plate and Syd Enever. (Courtesy John Seager)

The 'Classic Car Event' of 1988 came on 13 April, when British Motor Heritage, a subsidiary of the Rover Group, announced that it was going to put the right-hand drive MGB chrome-bumpered roadster bodyshell back into production, competitively priced at £1295, plus VAT. It had been in 1986 that the company looked at the time and cost involved in the renovation of an old bodyshell and realised that they could reduce it by up to a half if a new one was available. Fortunately they were able to locate practically all the original press tools and jigs for the shell's 240 panels. Consequently these bodies are not replicas but the genuine article, so arresting the decline in the numbers of MGBs on the road. (Courtesy British Motor Heritage)

British Motor Heritage director David Bishop (centre) supervises work on one of the new MGB bodyshells being undertaken at British Motor Heritage's factory in the town of Faringdon, Oxfordshire, just 11 miles from Abingdon. By a quirk of historical fate, when the MGB was in volume production the original bodies, produced at Pressed Steel's Swindon factory, had to be transported through Faringdon on their way for assembly. If the exercise proves a successful one, the rubber-bumpered, left-hand drive and GT MGB shells may also re-enter production. (Courtesy British Motor Heritage)

The spark of life: a bodyshell in preparation at BMH's works.

MGB
The illustrated history

The bodyshell was launched at *Classic Cars* National Classic Motor Show at the National Exhibition Centre Birmingham on April 30th/May 2nd 1988. There members of the public were able to witness the birth of a bodyshell which was subsequently completed and the resulting car took part in the 5th Regency Run from London to Brighton Run weeks later.

NOT TO SCALE

NUFFIELD WAY

ABINGDON
HOSPITAL

C

D

B

MARCHAM ROAD A415

A

PAVLOVA
WORKS

TO ABINGDON
TOWN CENTRE

CEMETERY

Larkhill

CEMETERY ROAD

SPRING ROAD

PL

CEMETERY

Parts of Hillier Parker's
brochure produced when the site was put
up for sale in 1981.

ABINGDON, OXFORD

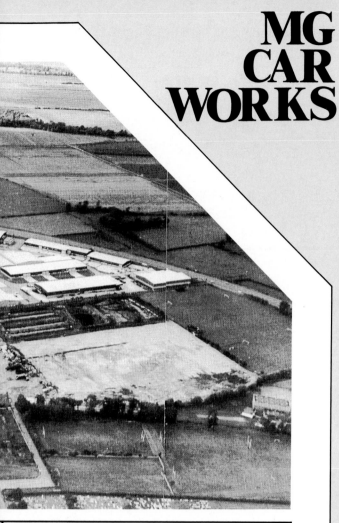

MG CAR WORKS

LOCATION
Abingdon is well situated on the A34 Trunk Road from Southampton which is a major route for freight traffic gaining access to Oxford and the Midlands.
M40 – 12 miles
M4 – 15 miles
London – 62 miles
Southampton – 60 miles
Bristol – 64 miles
Birmingham – 64 miles

TRANSPORT
Heathrow Airport is within one hours driving time from Abingdon and Birmingham International Airport is some 58 miles away. A train journey to London takes 59 minutes.

DESCRIPTION
The site is situated within half a mile of the junction of the A34 with the A415. Road access is gained via the main entrance on Marcham Road (A415) to the south, Nuffield Way to the west and Cemetry Road and Spring Gardens to the east. The complex has been built over a period of years and the most recent buildings were erected within the last ten years.
With an overall site area of 42 acres, the 410,000 sq. ft. of existing buildings are capable of further expansion up to 800,000 sq. ft. or more.

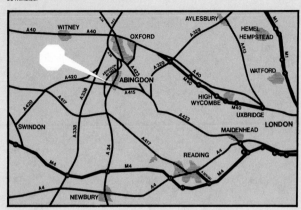

THE BUILDINGS
Block A
This building comprises ground floor, mezzanine, first and second floor accommodation incorporating the car assembly line, production stores, offices and ancillary workshops. The construction in the main is with brick wall surmounted by a steel truss roof on steel columns and beams. The roof is covered with slate and corrugated asbestos with an eaves height of 17 ft.

Block B
Nine inter-connecting modern units built of brick with corrugated asbestos and perspex roof supported on steel trusses. First floor and mezzanine accommodation contains offices, general stores, and toilet areas. The eaves height vary from 16 ft. to 24 ft. and access is provided to both sides of the building.

Block C
This recently constructed building is of steel frame construction with brick work surmounted by corrugated asbestos cladding to the side and roof. Storage accommodation at mezzanine level and part of the ground floor has been partitioned to provide offices. The eaves height is 20 ft.

Block D
A modern purpose built building containing the air pollution control centre, constructed of brick walls with a flat asphalt roof and timber frame windows. Vehicular access is provided at either end of the building.

Administration Block
A three storey brick built building with slate roof comprising offices, board room and toilet accommodation.

Ancillary Buildings
These include a large detached boiler house, various general store rooms, compressor house, fire station, toilets, sub-stations and security gate houses.

SITE
Various extensive areas of land presently used for car parking and car dispatch areas situated to the north of the site, which are suitable for further development. The site is totally enclosed by walls and chain link fences with entry control from three gate houses.

FLOOR AREAS
All dimensions are approximate.

	Sq. Ft.	Sq. Metres
A Block		
Ground Floor	173,250	16,095
First Floor	67,100	6,234
Second Floor	600	56
B Block		
Ground Floor	103,500	9,615
First Floor	7,500	697
Adjoining Buildings	3,400	316
C Block		
Ground Floor	27,100	2,518
First Floor	400	37
D Block	9,900	920
Adminstration Block	7,000	650
Fire Station, Paint Store & Terrapins	4,150	386
Boiler House, Compressor & Engine Test Areas	6,500	604
	410,400	38,128

SITE AREA
42 acres approximately. Plans supplied on request.

SERVICES
The industrial complex is well serviced to meet most industrial and warehousing requirements.

Gas
150 mm (6") main connected.

Electricity
3 sub-stations are located on site. A ring main supply of 11,000 volts is reduced to 415 volts, 3-phase with a maximum load of 2,300 KVA.

Fire Protection
Sprinkler system and smoke detectors are installed throughout the complex.

Water
A 75 mm (3") main supply for domestic water. Bore-hole extraction capacity is currently limited by licence and it is our clients intention to disconnect one of the pumps but the purchaser will be under an obligation to provide electricity and extract water from the remaining bore-hole for the benefit of Pavlova. A 150 mm (6") pipe to the sprinkler system is set by a cylindrical pressure tank of 6,666 gallon capacity, in addition to a tank of 19,140 gallon capacity.

Compressed Air
Three compressors and an air distribution system serve all buildings.

Heating/Ventilation
There are two oil fired boilers each with a capacity of 16,000 lbs per hour of steam at 100 psi. Heating is provided by radiant strip, heater battery with fans and plenum ducted air. Three oil storage tanks having capacities of 10,000, 19,250 and 29,800 gallons capacity respectively.

Fuel Facilities
Two underground tanks are situated adjacent to C Block providing 1,250 gallon petrol and 1,250 gallon diesel capacity. Four underground tanks are situated adjacent to the production area in Block A providing two tanks of 1,250 gallons and two tanks of 3,000 and 6,000 gallons capacity respectively.

TOWN PLANNING
The property is zoned industrial but we understand that the consideration would be given to warehousing Class 10 user.

TENURE
The property is Freehold subject to certain way-leaves and rights of way, which can be supplied on request.

TERMS
Terms are available on application.

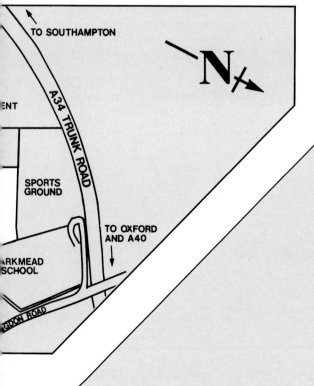

TO SOUTHAMPTON

N

A34 TRUNK ROAD

SPORTS GROUND

TO OXFORD AND A40

ARKMEAD SCHOOL

GDON ROAD

149

Chapter 3

Variations - The MGC *and* MGB GT V8

THERE WERE TWO attempts to market larger-engined versions of the MGB and both models failed to sell in respectable numbers but for completely different reasons. The 2.9 litre six-cylinder MGC was a controversial car from the moment of its announcement at the 1967 Motor Show. Yet if it had been 'right', as the MGB undoubtedly was, the GT version would have come closest to John Thornley's original inspiration of an Aston Martin DB 2/4 for everyman. It remained in production for just over two years and was *not* a popular model at Abingdon. The second attempt came in 1973 when the 3^1/$_2$ litre Rover V8 engine was ingeniously shoehorned under the MGB's bonnet with, remarkably, far fewer modifications required than for the fitment of the six. The MGB GT V8 was a fast, practical, if rather dated, car but its announcement came in a year that saw the outbreak of the Arab/Israeli war and the energy crisis that sprang from it, for although the V8 version of the B was an economical performer, maybe the very configuration frightened off potential purchasers. Also there were problems with the supply of Rover engines which contributed to a modest output and only a three year manufacturing life.

But first the MGC. A six-cylinder version of the MGB had been mooted at least six years before the car appeared. This is borne out by drawings made at Abingdon for parts of the car, dated January 1961, and that was a good 18 months before the announcement of the MGB. Also at about this time there were thoughts about a successor for the Austin Healey 3000 which dated back, in essence, to 1952 and had been built at Abingdon since 1957. It was decided therefore, that the six-cylinder version of the MGB should also be offered in Austin Healey form which echoed the smaller Midget/Sprite theme. The two projects were given respective ADO 52 and ADO 51 designations.

There was room under the MGB's bonnet for a six, the question was, which engine should be used to power the car? It was felt that by the time the new model went into production the C Series unit used in the Big Healey would be somewhat long in the tooth. The next thought was to fit the 2.2 litre Freeway six used by BMC Australia and one was fitted to a bronze GT for evaluation purposes. It was, in effect, one and a half B Series engines, but it was thought the unit had reached the limit of its development and although it performed well enough it was felt that there was not a big enough difference between its top speed and that of the standard MGB. Also, though its crankshafts were made at Longbridge, the engine was manufactured on the other side of the world which would have hardly represented an ideal state of affairs. (The tooling for this engine finally ended up with BMC's South African subsidiary).

But as the MGB benefited from the conception of the Austin 1800, so the MGC was able to use the redesigned C Series unit which was being produced for ADO 61, the Austin 3 litre saloon, announced simultaneously with the MGC, for the 1967 Motor Show. This north/south-engined rear wheel drive saloon was intended to replace the big Farina-styled Austin and Wolseley sixes which were beginning to show their years. This C Series rethink, like the B Series one undertaken for the 1800, mainly related to the unit's bottom end. Just as the four had its

Early thoughts: a scale model the early 1960s, the work of Don Hayter, of a six-cylinder MGB, featuring the then fashionable twin headlights and rear wing treatment echoing that of EX 205 of 1957.

The MGC roadster, as it appeared on its announcement in October 1967, looking virtually identical to its four-cylinder brother. The giveaways are the bonnet hump, to accommodate the larger radiator, and secondary bubble to allow the forward

three main bearings increased to five on NVH (noise, vibration, harshness) grounds, the same approach was adopted for the six with the four mains upped to seven.

The work was undertaken by Morris Engines at Coventry to Alec Issigonis's brief. Designated Type 29G when used in the MGC, the six retained the old C series 83 x 88mm bore and stroke and 2912 cubic capacity. The new mains were $1^{1}/4$ rather than $1^{3}/4$ inches wide and as there were seven of them the resistance they generated was an undoubted factor in the unit's reluctance to rev, a problem that had also been experienced with the previous four-bearing version. There were also alterations made to the positioning of the bores. The C Series

carburettor to clear the bonnet. Other differences are the 15 inch wheels, rather than the B's 14 inch ones. This roadster cost £1101, which was £153 more than the MGB equivalent.

had used three pairs of siamesed pots but during its redesign, water passages were introduced between each bore. Although this took up slightly more space, thinner and improved castings resulted in the new engine being $1^{3}/4$ inches shorter than the old. The cylinder head was similar to the C Series but the combustion chambers were relocated symmetrically to the centre line of the cylinders, instead of being offset on the exhaust side. Because the MGC's export

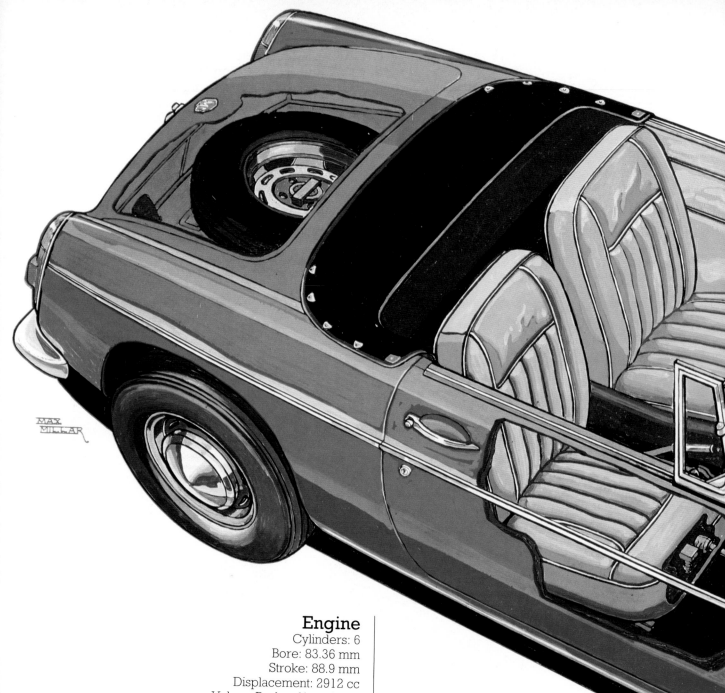

Engine

Cylinders: 6
Bore: 83.36 mm
Stroke: 88.9 mm
Displacement: 2912 cc
Valves: Pushrod/overhead
Compression ratio: 9:1
Carburettors: Twin SU 1.75 in type HS6
Power output: 145 bhp at 5250 rpm

Transmission

Clutch: 9 in Borg and Beck, single dry-plate
diaphragm
Gearbox: 4-speed, all synchromesh
Ratios: Overdrive cars 1967-69, Non-overdrive
1969, Top 1.0, 3rd 1.307, 2nd 2.058, 1st 2.98,
reverse 2.679. Pre-1969 non overdrive cars, Top
1.0, 3rd 1.382, 2nd 2.167, 1st 3.44, Reverse, 3.095
Overdrive: Optional, Laycock LH type, Top 0.82,
3rd 1.07
Automatic Transmission: Optional, three-speed
Borg-Warner Type 35, Top, 3.31, 2nd, 4.79, 3rd,
7.91, Reverse, 6.92

Final drive: Non-overdrive cars
to Chassis no 4235, 3.07.
Overdrive: cars to Chassis no 4235 and non-
overdrive cars from Chassis 4236; automatic
gearbox, 3.31. Overdrive cars from Chassis no
4236, 3.7

Chassis

Construction: Unitary
Brakes: Girling, servo-assisted
Front: 11.6 in disc
Rear: 9 x 2.5 in drum
Steering: Rack and pinion, 3.5 turns lock to lock
Suspension – front: Independent, torsion bar,
wishbone
Suspension – rear: Half elliptic, leaf spring
Wheels: Ventilated 5J x 15 disc.
Optional 5J wire wheels.

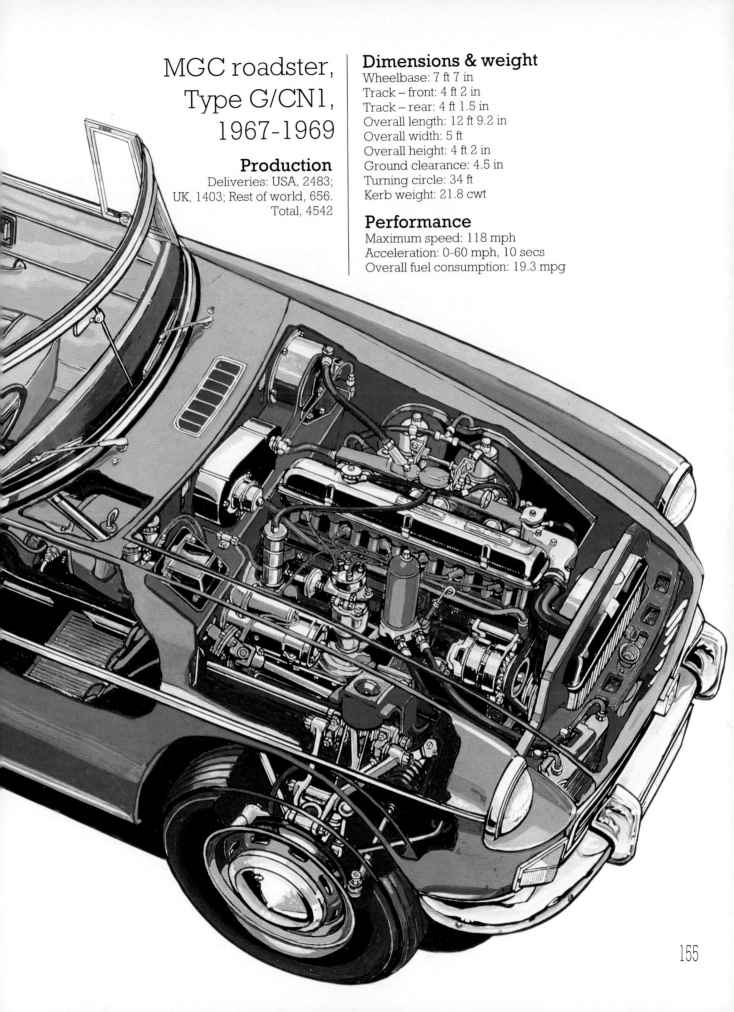

MGC roadster, Type G/CN1, 1967-1969

Production
Deliveries: USA, 2483;
UK, 1403; Rest of world, 656.
Total, 4542

Dimensions & weight
Wheelbase: 7 ft 7 in
Track – front: 4 ft 2 in
Track – rear: 4 ft 1.5 in
Overall length: 12 ft 9.2 in
Overall width: 5 ft
Overall height: 4 ft 2 in
Ground clearance: 4.5 in
Turning circle: 34 ft
Kerb weight: 21.8 cwt

Performance
Maximum speed: 118 mph
Acceleration: 0-60 mph, 10 secs
Overall fuel consumption: 19.3 mpg

potential had to be considered, provision was also made in the head for drillings between the inlet and exhaust ports for the fitment of EPAI (Exhaust Port Air Injection) for the all-important American market. Net output for the engine was 145 bhp at 5250 rpm which was five bhp *less* than the C Series engine it replaced. The new bearing layout and exhaust emission scavenging facility undoubtedly played their parts in producing this disappointing figure.

The MGC's 2912cc engine, similar to that used in the Austin 3 litre saloon announced simultaneously. The MG unit had a 9:1, rather than 8.2:1, compression ratio (though the 3 litre unit was soon brought into line with the MGC in that respect), twin 1.75 inch SU HS6 carburettors, different manifolding and camshaft. The brake servo was a standard fitting on the C, as was the oil cooler. Although the rocker box cover featured a black crackle

At Abingdon, the MGB was being modified to accept the engine and its new, all-synchromesh gearbox while an automatic version was also to be offered. This fitting required a considerable amount of structural surgery at the front of the car. The main difficulty was the depth of the new engine which was such that the MGB's front suspension cross-member could not be retained. It was replaced by a new one which mirrored the contours of the sump and swept up each side of the power unit to be incorporated in new inner wing panels which formed the engine compartment. This meant that the front suspension had to be completely redesigned and was unique to the model

finish, this was soon changed to a painted one as it proved to be almost impossible to keep clean. The C featured a sealed cooling system, with expansion tank, something that would not be fitted to the MGB until 1976.

and, for that matter, any other BMC car. There was a widely spaced upper wishbone while the lower member was a single link made up of two channel section forgings bolted back to back. This was connected to an adjustable longitudinal torsion bar that ran about halfway down the car. 'This effectively transmitted the suspension stresses back to the centre of the car where we introduced a heavy cross-member,' recalls Roy Brocklehurst who was responsible for the layout. For the king pins, hubs and bushes Roy remembers utilising existing components from the contemporary Austin Taxi! This new suspension required the introduction of telescopic shock absorbers with their upper ends mounted on the cross-member extensions. Lever arm units were retained at the rear. A front anti-roll bar was fitted although its diameter was increased by $1/8$ inch to $11/16$ inch. Rack and pinion steering was retained, though the unit's position was lowered so that it lined up with the lower wishbones. In view of the extra forward weight its ratio was lowered,

Looking down on the same engine, with the vertically mounted oil filter and Lucas 16AC alternator clearly visible. Note the cross-member, peculiar to the MGC, beneath the oil cooler pipes, to which the suspension was mounted; the top of the offside telescopic shock absorber is clearly visible.

The MGC's substantial six-cylinder, seven-bearing crankshaft engine out of the car, with its pre-engaged starter motor and complete with new all-synchromesh gearbox, which was also shared with the MGB. The gearbox employed a remote control gear lever, in contrast to when it was fitted in the MGB, which did not have such a facility. Note the rocker box is painted.

MGB
The illustrated history

the MGC having 3.5 turns lock to lock rather than 2.9 on the lighter B.

Brakes were Girling rather than the B's Lockheed units though, because the C was to be a faster car, larger $11^{11}/16$ inch diameter discs were fitted at the front though the rear drums were smaller than the Bs, being 9 inches rather than 10 inches diameter, but were $1/4$ inch wider. Servo assistance was

A close up of the MGC's gearlever, with the new short gearlever and round knob. This version is fitted with an LH type Laycock overdrive, available at £61 9s 2d. Like the unit fitted to the MGB, it operated on third and top gears.

standardised on the car. Wheels were also larger, being 15 rather than 14 inch, and had five in place of four stud mountings. All these modifications were made to an MGB using a wooden representation of the new engine/ gearbox unit. MG engineers were thus familiar with its dimensions and they were informed by Morris Engines that the redesigned C Series unit would weigh 495 lb, which was 137 lb more than the four-cylinder MGB one.

But when the 'new' engine finally arrived at Abingdon the MG team was horrified to find that it weighed no less than 567 lb, which was 72 lb, or over half a hundredweight more than Morris Engines told them it would be. John Thornley clearly remembers when the unit was first fitted to the prototype MGC: 'It made the car kneel down. It put the front suspension all to hell and although that problem was resolved the mass of the engine made the car want to go straight ahead when cornering. The redesign had saved precisely 44 lb in weight over the old C Series engine. The suspension problems were sorted out to a great extent by winding up the torsion bars to compensate for the increased weight and Roy Brocklehurst confirms that there was

The overdrive unit when fitted in the car, with the actuating solenoid unit on the right and part of the offside torsion bar on the left.

plenty of scope left in the bars to allow for this. The rear axle was the MGB's proven Salisbury type unit with a 3.07:1 final drive ratio and 3.31:1 when overdrive was fitted.

The problems that MG were experiencing with the C which, of course, were none of their doing, deeply disturbed Donald Healey, and his son Geoffrey, as they felt that the resulting vehicle was likely to be inferior to the MGB for which they had much respect. So, in the autumn of 1966, following Donald Healey's representations to BMC, ADO 51, the Austin Healey version of the MGC, was

158

abandoned as he did not wish his name to be associated with the project.

Although the prototype MGC had been completed in 1965, assembly of the first six pre-production cars didn't begin until 3 November 1966. They were chassis numbers 101, 102, 104, 108, 109 and 112. The car

sold around 10,000 before it was discontinued in 1971. With it went its controversial power unit, never to be used in another car.

Driving compartment of a left-hand MGC roadster with kilometers per hour speedometer. It is almost identical to that of the MGB and although the bonnet blip is a giveaway, the real indication is the large leather-covered steering wheel.

made its public début at the 1967 Motor Show, along with the Austin 3 litre, though the latter didn't stagger into production until the summer of the following year and only

Underside of the MGC, showing its unique wishbone and torsion bar independent suspension, the work of Roy Brocklehurst. The 11/16 inch anti-roll bar, 1/8 inch thicker than the one used on the B, can also be seen. The steering rack is also clearly visible; in view of the weight of the six-cylinder engine, it was lower-geared than the MGB's, the C having 3.5 turns lock to lock, compared with the B's 2.9 turns. The cross-member below the engine and longitudinal torsion bars are readily apparent.

159

Head-on view of left-hand drive European specification MGC roadster. Of the 8999 Cs built between 1967 and 1969, (4542 roadsters and 4457 GTs), just under half (2483 roadsters and 1773 GTs), were exported to America, while a further 1306 went to non-US markets. The remaining 3437 were sold in Britain.

Rear view of the left-hand drive C roadster, with the higher ground clearance and MGC badge on the boot lid, as the only giveaways.

This car is fitted with optional 72 spoke wire wheels, which cost an extra £30 14s 7d, while eared knock-off wheel nuts were still fitted to British specification cars.

The MGC in its finished state looked very similar to the MGB which belied the extensive restructuring of its front end. The most obvious difference was that the six-cylinder car had two bulges in its aluminium bonnet; the first, accentuated by a chrome strip, was to clear the radiator mounted well forward of its position on the B, while there was a second protruberance to allow for the forward of the two HS6 SU carburettors. The C also tended to look rather bigger than the B because of its 15 inch wheels which gave the model greater ground clearance. Only at the back of the car was the model's true identity revealed, with badges proclaiming MGC rather than MGB. Once behind the steering wheel, which was leather covered, interior differences were minimal. There were two-speed windscreen wipers, new door handles and window winders. The

A side view of the MGC GT, with standard disc wheels. It cost £1249 on its 1967 introduction, £155 more than its MGB equivalent.

MGC was priced at £1101 in open form while the GT sold for £1249, £153 and £156 respectively more than the four cylinder MGB.

In view of the problems MG had experienced with the creation of the MGC it comes as no surprise to find that *Motor* and *Autocar*, the respected British motoring weekly magazines, gave the new model a rather mixed reception. They recognised its long-legged qualities but disliked the engine's lack of low speed torque, its low geared steering and pronounced understeer.

Interior of a left-hand drive MGC GT, sharing the same leather-covered steering wheel as the roadster. Note safety-conscious window winder, a sign of the times, which was made of rubberised material, and intended to break off in the event of an accident.

Certainly the MGC had a 120 mph top speed which was around 20 mph faster than the MGB but how did the C's performance compare with the Austin Healey 3000 which it was intended, in part, to replace? When *Autocar* road tested a Mark III 3000 in 1964, it recorded a top speed of 121 mph and a 0-60 mph acceleration figure of 9.8 seconds, whereas the respective MGC figures were 120 mph and 10 seconds. The Healey was consistently faster than the C through the gears, did a standing quarter mile in 17.2 seconds, as opposed to 17.7, but weighed, at 2604 lb, over a hundredweight *more* than the MG's 2477 lb kerb weight. And it was thirstier, the MGC returning an overall petrol consumption figure of 17.5 mpg, as opposed to the 3000's 20.3 mpg. The only area where the MGC scored over the Big Healey was its price. Both cars were at the 1967 Motor Show (it was to be the 3000's last) the Mark III convertible, with overdrive, selling for £1126 while the open MGC was £25 less. Of course, the MG's defenders might argue that the C should not really be regarded as the Healey's successor. It was a rather more practical and refined vehicle but the fact that its engine was basically similar to the earlier car undoubtedly produced uncomfortable comparisons. Maybe in view of the model's bad press and a feeling amongst enthusiasts that the car had somehow lost the 'Abingdon touch', sales of the new car were disappointing. By the end of 1967 189 MGC roadster and 41 GTs had been built. These small numbers resulted

The same MGC GT viewed from the raised tailgate. Like the MGB, interiors by this time were black finished, with the exception of British Racing Green, Teal Blue and Bedouin body colours, which were trimmed in an Autumn Leaf hue.

from hold ups in the supply of engines from Coventry. Output for 1968, the first full year of production, saw production fairly evenly split between tourers and GTs with 2566 and 2462 respectively manufactured. In 1969, the year the model was phased out, there were slightly more closed cars built (1954) than roadsters (1787). The last cars were made at

Rear of a right-hand drive MGC GT, this time with wire wheels, with the MGC name on the tailgate.

The works hardtop was also available on the MGC at £73 15s extra. It is pictured here at a test day for motoring journalists at an inevitably wind swept Silverstone.

Abingdon on 4 August 1969 and the final MGC was a Primrose left-hand drive GT, which left the factory on 18 September. There was also a number of cars built during 1969, that had not been specifically ordered by dealers and which were offered by London MG distributors. University Motors purchased 156, some of which were fitted with potent Downton Conversions. The bulk of these MGCs were sold off as University Motors MG Specials.

So was the MGC as bad a car as the press and its contemporary reputation suggests? Today the car generates an enthusiastic following and, when I was on the staff of *Thoroughbred and Classic Cars,* I can recall Michael Bowler, the magazine's editor, enthusing about a 1968 MGC GT, which he used for commuting and long distance runs in 1978. His comments were undoubtedly interesting because he had been a member of the *Motor* road test team who had evaluated the car back in 1967. In T and CC

he wrote: 'The GT is a very practical sports car and quite nice looking; with its stiffer rear springs the C GT handles better ... The C engine has some virtues too; it is very quiet and remarkably smooth and torquey at the bottom end for relaxed top gear motoring. Even with adjustments it still doesn't get up and go but I still find the performance far more acceptable now than I did ten years ago ...'

Roy Brocklehurst, who was closely involved with the C's conception is characteristically forthright about the car: 'When we got that heavy engine it was just a matter of making the best of it. The C was a political nonsense, an understeering pig'. The last word on the MGC should go to John Thornley: 'It was a very good, long-legged car and if I had wanted to drive from Abingdon to Istanbul then there are few cars I would have rather gone in, provided there weren't too many corners!'

The next attempt to produce a larger

163

Under-bonnet view of MGC no G.52N 000584F, a left-hand drive car. Note that servo unit and pedal box have been transposed. The light green finish is also new. This car is destined for a non-American export market. Cars with an American destination were fitted with exhaust pollution equipment, different manifolding and separate circular air cleaners, in place of the single one shown here.

A blemish on the engine of a 1968 MGC being touched up by Bert Ellaway of the MG rectification department, located in Abingdon's C Block.

engined version of the MGB began with a phone call in 1971 to Roy Brocklehurst, by then MG's chief engineer. At the other end of the line was British Leyland's technical director Harry Webster. 'He wanted to know what I knew about Ken Costello.' (It was Costello, who in 1970, had begun producing conversions fitted with the alloy Rover V8

The ex-Buick 3528cc Rover V8, with its special MG rocker boxes, was a version of the Range Rover engine. Unlike the pioneering Costello car, which had a bonnet bulge, MG neatly got round the problem by creating a specially designed secondary chamber which permitted the twin SU HIF6 carburettors to be located adjacent to the bulkhead. In order to comply with exhaust emission legislation, particularly when the engine was cold, the bi-metallic valves shut flaps in the air intakes with the result that incoming air was warmed, via the exhaust manifolds. Other modifications included the fitting of a different alternator, while the adjacent oil filter was located in series with the oil cooler, rather than at the base of the oil pump. The twin thermostatically controlled electric fans can just be seen ahead of the radiator. The MGB's underbonnet structure was simultaneously altered in the interests of rationalisation.

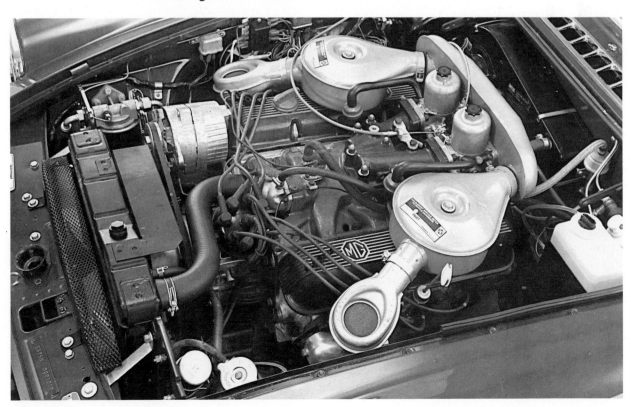

MGB
The illustrated history

engine). 'I told Harry I had seen one as Ken Costello came to Abingdon on occasions because he used to buy bits from Special Tuning'. Roy felt that the conversion was 'quite a desirable piece of merchandise but not terribly adequately engineered.' Harry Webster told Roy that Ken Costello wanted to buy his engine direct from Leyland and also wanted warranty on them once they were fitted in the MGB shell. Then he said 'If you were going to recommend changes that Costello should make, you'd have to produce a car! How long would it take you to do?' Roy told him 28 days and on the twenty-eighth he drove a converted white GT to Longbridge for British Leyland finance director John Barber, to borrow for the weekend. 'We had magnificent co-operation from Rover when it came to produce that first car,' remembers Brocklehurst. But, in view of the speed at which the conversion was undertaken, this experimental V8 had a bulge in its bonnet, to clear the engine's intrusive SU carburettors.

John Barber obviously liked the car because Brocklehurst received instructions to go ahead with a proper conversion. The work was undertaken, under Roy's direction, by Barry Jackson, son of Reg who'd been with MG since its Oxford days. The intention was to produce the car in GT form only. This was, according to Brocklehurst, because 'inherently the GT had greater torsional stiffness than the roadster'. And the conversion also appealed because it was relatively cheap to undertake, for there was none of the drastic surgery that had been necessary to create the MGC. But, inevitably there were some changes that had to be made to the B's engine bay. The inner wings were mildly reshaped to cope with the wider unit as were the chassis members that supported the engine. The bulkhead was also slightly altered to clear the end of the rocker boxes. A new radiator, capable of holding 16 rather than 9.5 pints of water, was introduced, though for space reasons twin electric fans were mounted *ahead* of the core. These under-bonnet modifications were simultaneously effected in the MGB.

This is one of the University Motors MG Specials, which the well-established London MG distributors marketed after the MGC ceased production in September 1969. Between then and November the company took delivery of 141 MGCs, 118 GTs and 23 roadsters. The cars are instantly identifiable by the new alloy slatted grille and matt black surround, similarly treated bonnet bulge and roof. Beneath the surface, the Cs were offered in various stages of Downton tune, University Motors having offered this facility, the work of the Westbury, Wilts based tuning concern, from the autumn of 1967. However, none of these MG Specials are exactly alike.

There was a number of limited changes made to the engine which was the low compression ratio 8.25:1 Range Rover unit rather than the 10.5:1 version used in the Rover 3500 and chosen because five star fuel's days were numbered and lower compression units were to be the order of the day. When used in the Range Rover, the engine's oil filter projected forwards and downwards but this would have fouled the MGB's anti-roll bar so the filter mounting was removed and a new casting made. Consequently the filter was repositioned on the right-hand inner wheel arch and connected in series with the oil cooler. The exhaust manifolds were also redesigned with shorter manifolding which drew them in closer to the body of the engine while the twin exhausts merged into one in the region of the car's bellhousing. In view of the lack of space, the engine's five-blade fan was dispensed with and replaced by electric units.

Then there was the problem of those

The V8's interior was much the same as the MGB's but with smaller 80mm diameter speedometer, calibrated up to 140 mph, and matching rev counter in place of the 4 inch diameter dials previously fitted. The three-spoke steering wheel was leather bound, with plain, broad spokes. The stalk nearest to the camera activated two-speed windscreen wipers and washers in addition to the overdrive which operated in top gear only.

1973 publicity photograph. The V8's suspension was modified to cope with the increased weight, 2260 lb compared with the MGB GT's 2427 lb. The front coil springs were uprated while the rear ones, instead of having the MGB GT's one main leaf and five auxiliary ones, had just three. The brakes were also uprated, and although the 14 inch wheels dictated the diameter of the Lockheed front discs remaining the same at 10.75 inches, their width was increased from 0.35 to 0.5 inches. A servo was employed as a standard fitting.

The V8 had a top speed of 120 mph plus with the V8 badges on the radiator grille and front wing as the only indication that this is not an MGB GT.

projecting carburettors (the Range Rover V8 had used Stromberg Zenith CD units but SUs were fitted when used in the MG). The bonnet bulge the SUs necessitated had marred the appearance of the original Costello MGB and Abingdon's first effort so Alec Hounslow, another MG veteran, came up with a neat solution. He used the original Rover inlet manifold as his primary chamber but then created a second one which repositioned the twin SU HIF6 carburettors at the rear of the engine where there was rather more under-bonnet space. These units breathed through a common air box, sandwiched between the carbs and the heater unit, which was in turn fed with twin air filters mounted on top of the engine's rocker boxes. The individual intakes were positioned directly above the exhaust manifolds, incorporating patented shut off flaps, to take advantage of preheated air. Despite this ingenious compromise, it was still necessary to give the V8's bonnet slightly increased curvature, a modification that was also shared with the MGB. (A similarly subtle modification was adopted when the bonnet of the Twin Cam MGA was slightly curved to clear the engine's cam boxes, and the new pressing was also extended to the pushrod cars that didn't really require it!)

The modified engine was given a new bellhousing that permitted the fitting of a $9^1/2$ inch rather than 8 inch diameter clutch. The gearbox internals were largely MGC and overdrive was standardised. It initially operated on top and third gears though, soon after production began, top only was served. Suspension modifications were limited to uprated front springs while at the rear, three stiff half-elliptics replaced the six leaves used on the MGB. In view of the greater performance forthcoming from the 3.5 litre V8, the front disc brakes were thickened up from .35 to .5 inches and a vacuum servo, still optional on the B, was standardised. The car also required its own rack and pinion steering unit. The only really distinctive external feature, apart from the rather discreet V8 badges on the radiator grille and tail gate, were the four-stud alloy wheels, with tyre size upped from 165-14 to 175-14. These were not specially made for the V8, Dunlop being in the process of offering them as an aftermarket fitment on the MGB. Inside, the V8 was almost identical to the MGB with the exception of a 140 mph speedometer and 6000 rpm

rev counter with a warning amber band set at 5250 rpm. The combined oil pressure/water temperature gauge was also new, the V8 running at unusually low pressure at 35 to 40 psi. Incredibly, the aluminium V8 was 40 lb lighter than the MGB's cast iron four but this advantage was offset by the weight of its ancillaries and the larger radiator. Therefore the new car weighed 2427 lb, compared with the B's 2260 lb. Top speed was around the 125 mph mark making the GT V8 the fastest production MG ever built. The engine developed 137 bhp (DIN) at 5000 rpm.

The first production V8 was completed on 12 December 1972 and work on a further 12 was started by the end of January 1973. Of these seven, chassis numbers 101, 102, 104, 105 and 108/9/10 were left-hand drive examples. They were fitted with special detoxed engines, there were nine power units in all, and the cars were shipped to America on an evaluation programme because there were thoughts of selling the model in the United States. Unfortunately the idea was stillborn because the amount of work that would have been necessary to modify a relatively small number of cars to the ever stringent Federal emission requirements would have been difficult to justify. So the seven GTs were returned to Abingdon and sold off from there.

The MGB GT V8 was announced in August 1973 when its price was set at £2294, which was £560 more than the MGB GT. It was also a good £500 more than the V6 Ford Capri 3000 GXL which cost £1824. The press seemed to like the car even though it was felt that the model had arrived too late in the day and the ride, wind noise and generally dated appearance were bound to count against it. Fuel consumption, however, was impressive. *Autocar* recorded 23.4 mpg overall which compared favourably with the MGB.

By the end of 1973, the first year of production, 1031 V8s had been produced, the peak month being October when 176 cars left Abingdon. Output held up well for the first five months of 1974. January saw 142 V8s produced and respective monthly totals until May were 145, 75, 124 and 122. But from June output began to dwindle with 94 built: 29 in July, 58 in August and 18 in September. It should be remembered, however, that at this time the rubber-bumpered MGB was entering production, so the plant's energies

MG
The illu

The second variation of the MGB theme was the MGB GT V8, available in GT form only, its announcement being embargoed until 15 August 1973. Externally it was similar to the four-cylinder car, with the exception of the Dunlop special alloy wheels with ventilated cast alloy centres. These began life on the Reliant Scimitar and were mildly modified for use by MG. They were first used by MG on its 1972 one-off Special Safety Vehicle (SSV 1), or EX 250 in Abingdon design parlance. The V8 and British Leyland badges were only fitted on the car's nearside front wing, unlike the MGB, which had them on both. Sundym tinted glass was a standard fitting. Door-mounted wing mirrors were also fitted. The model was only produced in right-hand drive form because it was not exported to America.

were no doubt absorbed with this all-important modification.Total production for the year amounted to 882 V8s. Nineteen seventy-five was rather worse, with monthly production never exceeding 93, that peak being attained in April. October and November were the worst months with one car only manufactured in each. Output tailed off badly by the time production came to an end in 1976 with just 188 V8s built; the last example was made in September. This made a total of 2591 built during the three year production run.

So why did this version of the MGB not sell in larger numbers? One factor seems to have been a shortage of engines. 'We just couldn't get enough of them. The most we ever managed was 48 in one week,' recalls Don Hayter who was chief engineer at Abingdon at the time of the V8's production.

Another consideration was the timing of the model's announcement. The Arab/Israeli war broke out towards the end of 1973 and petrol prices shot up in its wake. This was

Although the MGB GT V8 was not sold in America, it had to be fitted with the polyurethane bumpers that were used by all MGB's from the 1975 model year, with the consequent loss of the V8 badge on radiator grille. This is a 1976 model year car (note the GT badge behind the side window, introduced on all GTs at the time), but it was destined to be the last year of V8 production. Only 489 cars had been built in 1975 and a mere 188 were produced in 1976. The model was officially discontinued in July but single examples were built in August and September.

hardly a healthy environment for selling an ageing relatively pricey 2 + 2 V8-engined car, however economical it might have been. If the model had been marketed two or three years earlier then the story might have been a different one.

Alex Hounslow, right foreground, MG's chief development engineer, who retired in October 1974, pictured with Don Hayter on the occasion of his retirement. One of Hounslow's last assignments at Abingdon was to create the special inlet manifold on the V8 engine which avoided the unsightly bonnet bulge which had marred the appearance of the Costello V8. The MG design and development team is in the background. The car, JBL 308L, and known as Flame 99, was the first pre-production right-hand drive car. There was incidentally, a left-hand drive equivalent, created in the hope that the model could be sold in America. (Courtesy Don Hayter).

Demolition. The old Pavlova Leather Company's gas engine house, used for a time by the MG development department being demolished in 1981. However, much of the old factory still survives with A, B and C Blocks all remaining. (Courtesy John Seager)

Chapter 4

Competition MGB & MGC

IN THE PUBLIC mind, the MG marque has been consistently identified with racing so it may come as a surprise to find that official works teams only existed on two separate occasions. The first was in 1955 when there was a brief period of track racing. Fortunately the introduction of the MGB saw the company return to the competitive fray and this was maintained until the Leyland take-over of 1968. Although the MGB's competition activities were never outstandingly successful, the cars were consistent performers and helped maintain the Safety Fast image in the minds of the motoring public.

As recounted earlier, the appearance of the MGA in EX 182 guise at Le Mans in 1955 marked an inspired return to official MG competitive activities. However, the commitment was a short-lived one after bad crashes there and at the Tourist Trophy race at Dundrod and BMC deemed that the emphasis should be thereafter switched to rallying. There was a trickle of entries, mostly at Sebring, USA and a works participation at Le Mans though the MGA in question was ostensibly entered by the North Western Centre of the MG Car Club but prepared at Abingdon for Ted Lund to race in 1959/61.

In September 1961 Stuart Turner took over as BMC Competitions Manager from Marcus Chambers who had held the post since 1954. The following year, which saw the launch of the MGB, a team of three special cars (chassis numbers 3698, 3699 and 3700) was prepared for racing. These cars closely resembled production cars with the EX 182 theme maintained by the use of aluminium bodywork, though extra lights and perspex cowls over the headlamps were fitted. Under the bonnet, purpose-built engines, prepared by the Morris Engines Coventry works, were employed with special camshafts and a single Weber 45 DCOE carburettor used in place of the production twin SUs. Compression ratio was upped from 8 to 11:1. The exhaust system was also special with the pipe emerging from under the passenger's door. A close-ratio gearbox and lightweight seats also featured.

The cars, (6/7/8 DBL), finished in red with white hardtops, received their competition baptism at the Sebring 12 hour race in March 1963, an event in which MGs had participated since it was initiated in 1952. Unfortunately the MGBs' début was an unsuccessful one as all the cars ran their bearings, the Florida climate contrasting starkly with the arctic like conditions prevalent in Britain that had prevented exhaustive testing of the cars. One of the Bs (6 DBL) was sold after the race but another, (7 DBL), redeemed itself with a GT class win at the *Daily Express* International Trophy meeting at Silverstone in May. This same car was then prepared for that year's Le Mans 24 hour race, the first MG entry at Sarthe since Ted Lund's 1961 sortie. The 1963 entry featured 7 DBL with a distinctive cowled nose to improve air flow and similar in profile to Lund's 1961 car. Twin fuel tanks were fitted, along with an ultra high 3.307:1 final drive ratio. Top speed was in the region of 130 mph plus. Even though the B was a works car, BMC management felt that it should be 'privately' entered. Alan Hutcheson and Paddy Hopkirk shared the wheel and despite an unscheduled 1 1/2 hour stop when Hutcheson had to dig himself out of the sand on the Mulsanne Straight, 7 DBL finished the race in twelfth overall position,

Previous page, top: Abingdon prepared three MGB competition cars in 1963, registered 6 DBL, 7 DBL and 8 DBL. This is 6 DBL, one of the two works MGBs entered for the 1963 12 Hour International Sports Car Race at Sebring, Florida in March, which was the model's first international race. The intention was to provide MG with all-important publicity as a spur to MGB sales in America, and works cars were entered there every year until 1968. Modifications on the 1963 cars included aluminium front wings, doors, and boot lid, lightweight seats, and cowled headlamps, while the hardtop concealed an anti-roll bar. The MGB team, finished in scarlet with cream hardtops, consisted of a second car (7 DBL) together with a spare one. The race, alas, was soon over for both cars, driven by Christabel Carlisle and Denise McCluggage and Americans Jim Parkinson and Jack Flaherty, when oil surge resulted in their all running their big-ends.

Previous page bottom: The engine compartment of an MGB, as prepared for the 1963 Sebring race. The more obvious modifications are the special inlet manifold and attendant side-draught twin-choke Weber carburettor. Heater trunking conveys cooling air from the front of the car to the engine compartment. The heater unit has been removed and the battery was subsequently fitted in its place.

Inset, top: The MGB entered for the 1963 Le Mans race; a works car, 7 DBL, but fitted with an aluminium nosepiece, said to be worth 6 mph, with perspex cowled headlamps. It was 'entered' by Alan Hutcheson because BMC publicly distanced itself from racing at this time. He co-drove with Paddy Hopkirk and although Hutcheson had the misfortune to run into the Mulsanne sand, and spent one hour and 25 minutes digging out, the car finished in twelfth position, having averaged 91.96 mph. (Courtesy Quadrant/Autocar)

The Hutcheson/Hopkirk MGB, with the 250P Ferrari of Surtees/Mairesse in front of the Elde/Dumay GT of the same make, which was placed fourth, at Mulsanne early on the Sunday morning of the 1963 Le Mans race. Note the marks of wide cornering during the night. (Courtesy Quadrant/Autocar)

7 DBL
during the 1963
Le Mans race going
through the Esses
and being baulked by
the Sala/Rossi Alfa
Romeo SZ. (Courtesy
Quadrant/Autocar)

MINSK
29 voitures

MONTE-CARLO
37 voitures

8 DBL, another of the works MGBs, causing a stir in Skopjie, Yugoslavia, in August 1963, while workmen endeavour to cope with the devastation caused by an earthquake in July, which made 100,000 people homeless. The event was the Spa-Sophia-Liège Rally and the MG, driven by David Hiam and Rupert Jones, survived until the demanding section between Skopjie and Titograd, when specially fabricated rear springs fractured, putting the car out of the event. (Courtesy Quadrant/Autocar)

A French entered MGB, driven by Houel and Jacquin, one of 29 starters which began the 1964 Monte Carlo Rally from Minsk in Russia. The B did not, alas, complete the course though the Hopkirk/Liddon Mini Cooper S, which also started from Minsk, won the event. (Courtesy Quadrant/Autocar)

averaged 91.96 mph and achieved second place in the 1600 to 2000cc class behind the Barth/Linge Porsche. Overall miles per gallon was 14.13. This same car was driven by Andrew Hedges in the ten day Tour de France Rally but, unfortunately, crashed when in fourth position overall.

The first event of 1964 was the Monte Carlo Rally when a rejuvinated 7 DBL, driven by Donald and Erle Morley, won the 1601/2500cc class in the GT section, an event, incidentally, which saw Paddy Hopkirk in a Mini Cooper S win, thus upholding BMC laurels. 7 DBL was finally written off with the Morley twins again

However, Don and Erle, the Morley brothers, in 7 DBL, the works B, who started from Oslo, won the 1601 to 2500cc Grand Touring Class in the 1964 rally and are pictured on the Monte Carlo waterfront. (Courtesy Quadrant/Autocar)

MGB
The illustrated history

driving, after crashing in the Scottish Rally in May. Three new cars were prepared for 1964 and the MGB regained credibility at Sebring with a third in class placing. The Le Mans car (BMO 541B) was driven by Paddy Hopkirk and Andrew Hedges and, like the previous year's car, was specially prepared for the event. The engine was over-bored to 1801cc and with a 10.4:1 compression ratio developed around 125 bhp at 6000 rpm. The fuel tank was a 20.5 gallon one with its filler projecting through the boot lid, while 5.50 x 16 R6 Dunlop tyres were fitted. Keen-eyed observers in the paddock noticed that one of BMO 541B's front wings had been borrowed from another works MGB, the names of Sprinzel and Hedges just showing through the red paintwork! Fortunately the car ran without a major hitch, the only one being when a *plombeur* inadvertently dropped the car's petrol cap during re-fuelling at about 8.30 on the Saturday evening which knocked its all important ears off. A wire lash-up was approved which lasted for around two and a half hours. In the meantime a Sunbeam Tiger retired which, by chance, shared the same cap as the MGB. This was hastily transferred to the MG, the Sunbeam team manager being none other than Marcus Chambers, who it will be recalled, had looked after BMC's competition interests between 1954 and 1961. Maybe it was this hold-up that caused BMO 541B to record a tantalising 99.945 mph average speed, missing the magic 100 mph by a whisker. Nineteenth overall place was achieved and the MG won the *Motor* trophy for the first British car home. As in the previous year, the Le Mans entry also competed in the Tour de France of three months later but had to retire.

The 1965 racing season again kicked-off with Sebring and with two cars entered; one achieved a class second and the other completed the course. MG morale received a boost in May when John Rhodes and Warwick Banks in 8 DBL achieved an outright win in the Brands Hatch 1000 Miles Race. Hopkirk and Hedges again upheld MG laurels at Le Mans in a new car DRX 255C, finishing in eleventh position, the highest

MGBs were campaigned by private owners in countless races, rallies and trials the world over. Here the owner of a left-hand drive MGB is participating in the 1964 Alpenfahrt.

This MGB, registered BMO 541B, was officially entered for the 1964 Le Mans 24 hour race. It was fitted with the same aerodynamically efficient nose, which closely followed the profile of the EX 181 record breaker, to the one that 7 DBL had used in the same event in the previous year. Other more obvious departures from standard include the recognition light on the hardtop and the one illuminating the race number on the door. The front and rear white painted brackets, for quick release jacks, were so coloured to show up at night.

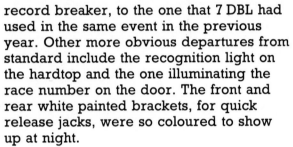

Rear view of the 1964 Le Mans MGB, with the exhaust pipe emerging just ahead of the rear wheel. Note that the car is bumperless, has an interior roll-over bar, and is registered for the road. Dunlop R6 racing tyres are fitted.

The boot of the Le Mans car with auxiliary petrol tank making a total of 20.5 gallons, with quick-release filler, which projected through the boot lid when closed. Boot lid and bonnet were strapped down. Twin SU fuel pumps were fitted.

post-war placing achieved by the marque at the Sarthe circuit. The pair averaged 98.24 mph for the 24 hours with a fuel consumption of 13.27 mpg. However, they missed the *Motor* trophy, the Rover BRM gas turbine car having come in ahead of them in tenth position. They also achieved second in class. This was to be MGs last entry at Le Mans because the car was being progressively outclassed and an all-time best eleventh placing was, perhaps, the right note on which to depart.

Fuelling the 1964 Le Mans MGB at the circuit, prior to scrutineering, watched by Paddy Hopkirk, while *Safety Fast*'s editor, Wilson McComb, right, looks on.

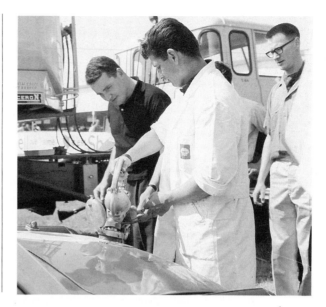

By the time that the car had got to Le Mans it had acquired its BMO 541B number plate. Here the MG is being inspected by race officials, a procedure that took place at the circuit from 1961. Prior to that, scrutineering was undertaken in the town of Le Mans.

Paddy Hopkirk (left) and Andrew Hedges pose with the B prior to the race. Pit manager Peter Browning specified a rev limit of 6500 rpm in third gear and 6000 rpm in top. The car averaged 14 mpg throughout the event. Note that only one windscreen wiper is fitted.

Contrast this photograph with the previous one, as it was taken during the race with

Hopkirk wasting little time in getting back into the B after a pit stop. A Microcell driver's seat was fitted.

Le Mans 1964. The Hopkirk/Hedges works B holding its own with the Rene Bonnet Aerodjet of Farjon and Lelong, placed 23rd and the Massan, Zeccoli Alpine Renault M63, right, which came in 20th, behind the MGB. (Courtesy Quadrant/Autocar)

The car ran faultlessly throughout the race, reached 104 mph on its best lap and achieved close on 140 mph down the Mulsanne Straight. It won the *Motor* trophy for the highest placed British-built and entered car.

Another private MGB entrant, this time on the 1964 RAC Rally. Driven by R.H. Parr and T.J. Oldham, this enthusiastic duo did not, alas, feature in the results.

MGBs put up an excellent showing in the Guards 1000 Mile Race, held over the weekend of 22/23 May 1965. 8 DBL, the victorious works MGB, was prepared and entered by Don Moore and driven by John

Rhodes and Warwick Banks. The event consisted of two heats, the first held on the Saturday, and was won by the Rhodes/Banks MGB, with Trevor Taylor and his sister Anita second in an ex-works B, while John Sach and Roger Enever, son of chief engineer Syd, in another B secured fifth place. The Taylor car gave 8 DBL a tough time in the second heat but the latter came in fourth on aggregate and won the event, the longest motor race to be held in Britain since the war.

The Rhodes/Banks works MGB showing its worth in the 1965 Guards 1000 Miles Race at Brands Hatch, with Austin Healey 3000 on the left, and a brace of E-type Jaguars behind. (Courtesy Quadrant/Autocar)

The Jackie Oliver/Chris Craft 4.2 litre E-type Jaguar, which was placed third overall, just ahead of the Rhodes/Banks MGB in the 1965 Guards 1000, with the JCB-entered ex-works MGB of Anita and Trevor Taylor behind. (Courtesy Quadrant/Autocar)

MGB
The illustrated history

The Taylors' ex-works MGB, that gave the factory car such a run for its money in the 1965 Guards 1000. Although it lead for a time on aggregate in the second heat, after 120 laps the rival works MGB was just

Yet another three special MGBs were prepared for the 1966 season. At Sebring two cars were entered. One was bored out to 2004cc and eventually threw a connecting rod, while the other went on to win the 2 litre class and was the third GT home. The Brands Hatch 500 Mile event was opened to larger capacity Group 4 cars, so MG had to content itself with a creditable third placing behind Shelby American Cobra and GT40. At the same time two works MGBs were taking part in the 50th Targa Florio Rally. Timo Makinen and John Rhodes not only achieved a ninth overall placing but with GRX 307D won not only the 2 litre class but also the GT section, regardless of engine capacity. The Spa 1000 kilometer event also saw an MGB class win for the Targa Florio car. Even more impressive was an outright win in the Spa-Sofia-Liège Rally when MBL 546E driven by Andrew Hedges, Tony Fall and Julien Vernaeve regained the road after crashing. A second MGB, driven by Roger Enever and Alec Poole, only dropped out on the seventy-nineth hour of the 84 hour event when in second place with a broken half shaft. This was, in effect, an MGB's last big victory in an international competitive event though the cars continued to appear in

ahead. Then, at 6.40 pm, Taylor lost a core plug, while lying second, though this was rectified, but then its rear wheel collapsed on the last lap, so thwarting a very brave effort.

Top right: MG's 1965 Le Mans entry, looking similar to the previous year's car, though with aluminium doors, rear wings, bonnet and boot, the entire car, with fuel, weighing 2081 lbs, and was again driven by Paddy Hopkirk and Andrew Hedges.

Right: The same car at the 1965 Le Mans race in front of its pit. Note that additional lamps have been fitted. The three-bearing crankshaft engine was much the same as the 1963 and 1964 Le Mans entries. It was bored out 20 thou, to 1801cc, with a 10.4:1 compression ratio, high lift camshaft and Weber 45 DCOE twin-choke carburettor. As a result, the engine developed 125 bhp at 6100 rpm. It also had an oversized sump and oil pump, close ratio gearbox and 3.3:1 rear axle ratio.

competitions of a less significant nature. However, an all steel GT, driven by the successful duo of Paddy Hopkirk and Andrew Hedges, achieved a class win at the 1967 Sebring event.

Right: DRX 255C during the 1965 Le Mans race, behind the Bonnier/Piper Ferrari 635, which dropped out on the ninth lap.

Main picture: Paddy Hopkirk applies opposite lock through Arnage in the 1965 Le Mans race, the marque's final appearance at Sarthe, when it finished eleventh, the best ever performance by a works MGB in the 24 hour classic. (Courtesy Quadrant/Autocar)

Inset, top: The Hopkirk/Hedges MGB looks high and angular through the Esses at Le Mans in 1965 behind one of a trio of Alfa Romeo TZ2s. However, none of the Italian cars finished the event. Note that, like the MGB, the TZ is registered for the road, its UD prefix indicating the Italian town of Urdine where the Alfa Romeo competition department was located, while the B's RX suffix is a Berkshire registration because MG's Abingdon home was in the royal county, though, today, boundary changes have resulted in the town now being situated in Oxfordshire. (Courtesy Quadrant/Autocar)

Inset, bottom: The MGB completes the 1965 Le Mans race in eleventh position, which marked MG's final appearance at Sarthe. It is followed by the Thuner/Lampien Triumph Spitfire which was thirteenth. The MG's average speed of 98.24 mph was less than that of the previous year on account of its having been fitted with R7 Dunlop racing tyres, which were slightly wider than the R6s of the previous year, and one punctured after seven and a half hours. Subsequently a set of used R6s were fitted instead and the drivers were instructed to slow down slightly to ensure that they lasted the race. (Courtesy Quadrant/Autocar)

Left: Preparing works cars for the 1966 Monte Carlo Rally at Abingdon. In the foreground is Tony Fall's MGB with non-standard 1.75 inch twin SU carburettors while a gas-flowed cylinder head and high-lift camshaft were also fitted. Other modifications were close-ratio gearbox and low axle ratio. Note the roll-over bar and hardtop behind. In the background is the Mini Cooper S, driven by Paddy Hopkirk and Henry Liddon, which was placed third in the event, behind two other Mini Cooper Ss.

Bottom left: The Tony Fall car, all set for the 1966 Monte Carlo Rally. He started at Rheims, but dropped out following the first special stage after the steering column had chafed through one of the oil cooler pipes.

GRX 307D, later to be known as 'Old Faithful', experienced an unceremonious début in the 1966 Monte Carlo Rally for Tony Fall and Ron Crellin. Here the luckless passenger endeavours to get the car out of a snow drift near Saurat, France. (Courtesy Quadrant/Autocar)

Although 8 DBL was three years old in 1966, it was one of the works cars prepared for that year's Sebring 12 hour race. The perspex headlamp covers were by then a well established Sebring feature. The oil cooler can be seen just behind the radiator grille while the bonnet release catch is just above the left-hand side light. The nearside air intake directed cooling air into the engine compartment, while its oppposite number was fed into the car's interior and did the same for the driver.

A privately entered MGB participating at the Grand Sports Car Club's Brands Hatch meeting on Easter Monday 1964. (Courtesy Motor)

Sarthe Swansong: the Hopkirk/Hedges MGB in the 1965 Le Mans race. (Courtesy Geoff Goddard)

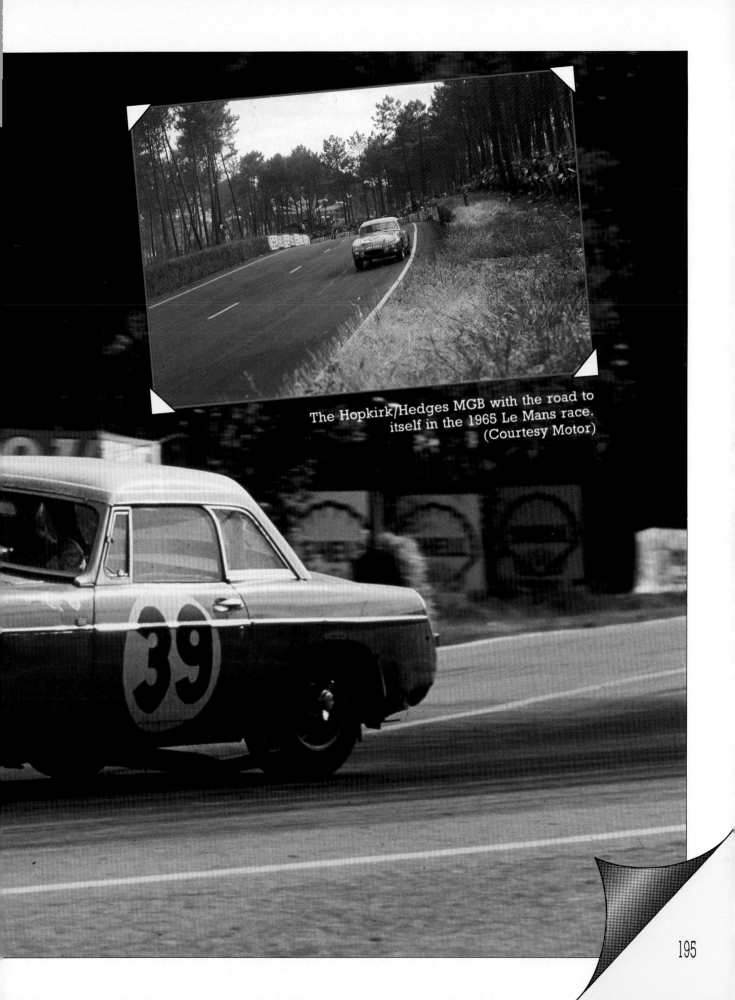

The Hopkirk/Hedges MGB with the road to itself in the 1965 Le Mans race. (Courtesy Motor)

MGB
The illustrated history

Under 8 DBL's bonnet, with Nobby Hall, an MG competition mechanic, in attendance. The engine was over-bored to 2004cc so that it could compete in the prototype class and ran on a single twin-choke Weber carburettor. It developed 138 bhp in this form.

From thereon the cars that took over the MG competitive torch were two special GTs, based mechanically on the new MGC which was announced in 1967. These were known at Abingdon as the GTS model and coded EX 241 in the MG design register. Six bodies were produced by Pressed Steel and employed a steel underframe to which light alloy panels were secured with rivets and liberal quantities of Araldite. Don Hayter was responsible for revamping the GTs shell in aluminium sections, and remembers spending many hours with Pressed Steel's Dave Nicholas seeing the project through. Although the cars still resembled the distinctive GT shape, the flared front and rear wheel arches showed that they meant business. Suspension was MGC-based with lon-

gitudinal torsion bars at the front which were adjustable from inside the car. There were additional locating arms for the rear axle and adjustable shock absorbers featured all round. Other departures from standard were a 24 gallon petrol tank with massive filler, Girling disc brakes on all four wheels (rather than just on the front) and alloy wheels on the knock on hubs. The first car, MBL 546E was built in 1967 but initially used a 2004cc *four*-cylinder engine because the MGC's announcement was not due until October. The car was entered in the Targa Florio as an MG GT, with the *B* noticeably lacking, when Paddy Hopkirk and Timo Makinen achieved a creditable third in class placing.

It wasn't until Sebring of 1968 that the

8 DBL's driving compartment, with modified facia and screenwash, fog lamp and demister controls in the centre, while the aluminium-spoked steering wheel is another departure from standard. Driven in the 1966 Sebring race by the seasoned team of Paddy Hopkirk and Andrew Hedges, time was lost in repairing a broken rocker shaft and while it was leading its class, with an hour and a half to go, it threw a connecting rod. However, the other works entry, HBL 129D...
...which was driven by Roger Mac, Peter Manton and Emmett Brown, completed 178 laps and finished in seventeenth position, won the 2 litre class and was placed third in the GT category. (Couresy Quadrant/Autocar)

MGB
The illustrated history

In May 1966 the Brands Hatch event was 500 rather than a 1000 miles, and Roger Enever and Alec Poole put up a stirling performance in the works MGB, 2 GLL. It is seen here in the pits during the race, in which it ran with clock-like reliability, and put up an excellent showing in the face of superior power of the Ford GT40, Sunbeam Tiger and Ferrari 275 LM. It held second place to a GT40 until late in the day but was overtaken by the Ford and came in third. The event was won by a Shelby-American Cobra. The B, however, achieved a class win, having completed the 167 laps at an average of 73.38 mph. (Courtesy Quadrant/Autocar)

Ancient and modern: the rapid advances in continental sports car design is dramatically highlighted in this photograph of the Enever/Poole works MGB, in the BOAC 500 Miles Race at Brands Hatch in July 1967. It is seen here being overtaken by the Ferrari 330P4 of Chris Amon and Jackie Stewart, which was placed second, ahead of the then novel be-winged Chaparral of Mike Spence and Phil Hill, which won the event. (Courtesy Quadrant/Autocar)

GTS appeared with its 2968cc six-cylinder engine in the manner of the MGC, the power unit showing the results of Abingdon's experience with the Austin Healey 3000 unit. Its capacity was achieved by 0.040in of overboring and with triple twin choke Weber carburettors fitted, the power unit developed in excess of 200 bhp at 6000 rpm.

Peter Brown and Tony Fall drove this privately entered MGB in the 1968 Targa Florio. Fall's practice time was the fastest of any British car. Despite two crashes they were also plagued by the car's gear lever, which kept disappearing through the floor because of a broken gearbox cross member. But they managed to keep going and came in 24th. (Courtesy Geoff Goddard)

GRX 307D, complete with ventilated hardtop, known as 'Old Faithful' at Abingdon, pictured in July 1966, in the Mugello road race. Driven in this Italian event by Andrew Hedges and Robin Widdows, it was placed third behind two GTB Ferraris.

DRX 255C, which ran at Le Mans in long-nosed form in 1965, pictured at Abingdon in 1967. It was damaged *en route* to Italy for a Mugello event, and again in the race itself, and was subsequently bought by Alec Poole, son of MGs Dublin importer, who rebuilt it using a jig supplied by the factory. Since about 1971 it has been owned by Barry Sidery-Smith and is in extremely original condition, complete with the steel front wing fitted after the Mugello incident.

Although the cylinder block was iron, an alloy cylinder head was used. The new car achieved a best ever result at Sebring and was placed in tenth position. In May came the Targa Florio and this time a rather more standard MGB GT, driven by Hopkirk and Hedges, won the sports car category and finished twelfth overall and was the first British car home.

A second GTS (RMO 699F) had been completed by August 1968 and this was entered along with the first one for the 84

The one and only competition MGB GT, LBL 591E, was specially prepared for the 1967 Sebring race with large petrol tank and roll-over bar. Note the marker and race number lights. It ran in the prototype class in 2004cc form and, driven by the redoubtable Hopkirk/Hedges duo, it finished in eleventh place and won its class. The same car ran in the 1968 Targa Florio when it finished second in the GT category.

'Old Faithful' in a similar state of preparation, pictured at Abingdon prior to the 1967 Sebring event. Enlarged to 1824cc, it was driven by Timo Makinen and John Rhodes, and was placed twelfth overall, third in the GT class.

BRX 855B, again driven by the proven team of Roger Enever and Alec Poole, ran in the 1967 Nurburgring 1000 kilometre race in May and kept going to achieve a third place in the 2 litre GT class. (Courtesy Quadrant/Autocar)

The GTS, or EX 241, of 1967, the first of two lightweight racing MGCs, the second being registered RMO 699F. Although the cars featured a steel underframe, use was made of light alloy sub structures, along with alloy body panels. MGC torsion bar front suspension was employed though as the model had not yet been announced. It ran in four-cylinder form and was enlarged, Sebring fashion, to 2004cc with twin SU carburettors rather than the usual single Weber, and developed 150 bhp at 6000 rpm. It ran in the Targa Florio, in May 1967 in this 'MGB GT' form, where it was placed third in its class for Group 6 cars over 2000cc, behind two Porsches, and was placed ninth overall.

MGB
The illustrated history

hour Marathon de la Route event at Nurbur-gring. Driving of the ex-Sebring car was shared by Andrew Hedges, Julien Vernaeve and Tony Fall. It did well, being in third position but, with 17 hours to go, trouble loomed. Unfortunately its front disc pads developed excessive wear and the excess

heat generated resulted in their welding themselves on. Because pit stops were limited to 20 minutes, the offending parts were removed and Tony Fall was, incredibly, sent out without brakes and continued for a further 21 laps until he stopped again for them to be re-installed. These heroic efforts resulted in the car finishing the race in sixth position overall. The other car,

Right: **The driving compartment of the 1967 lightweight MGC, complete with carpeted interior, and angled gearlever and rev counter.**

A line up of BMC cars pictured prior to the 1968 Sebring race. Left to right: a prototype Austin Healey Sprite, with 1293cc Lucas fuel-injected engine; the sole works MGB GT; an Austin Healey Sprite converted by Healey, at BMC's request, in to an MG Midget — they were looking for publicity in the US for the small MG for the sports car category; and the lightweight MGC, appearing, at last, in its true guise. All cars completed the race. Clive Baker and Mike Garton drove the fuel-injected Sprite and won the 1300cc prototype class but problems with water in the fuel resulted in their being placed 35th overall. The MGB GT was eighteenth overall and fifth in class, while the 'Midget' was fifteenth and won the sports car category. The MGB achieved a creditable tenth placing overall.

Left: Sebring Swansong: MBL 546E fitted with its racing MGC engine, showing the different bonnet contours, pictured prior to the 1968 Sebring race, complete with BMC rosette and Union Jack on the front wing. Driven by Hopkirk and Hedges, its tenth overall placing was the best result ever attained by a BMC car at the Florida circuit. It won its class and was also placed third in the prototype category. The same car also ran in the 84 hour Marathon de la Route at the Nürburgring in August of the year, along with RMO 699F, the second GTS, which retired with overheating. MBL 546E, brakeless in the latter stages of the event, following the front discs having welded themselves to the pads, eventually finished in sixth place, behind a bevy of Porsches. It was the last occasion in which a works sponsored MG appeared in a motor race.

With the creation of British Leyland in 1968, the lightweight GTSs were sold and the Abingdon-based competition department only lasted until 1970. The two lightweight cars, and the works MGB GT, were sold to MG's American importers and ran in the 1969 Sebring event finishing 15th, 24th and 28th. Parts of the third car, and the three remaining lightweight shells, the six were numbered GCD 000101L to GCD 000106L, were sold to John Chatham of Bristol. Chatham retained the partially dismantled car for Modsport racing and built up the remaining three shells. They were prepared for the road and registered VHW 330H, EHW 441K and this is VHY 5H, which Chatham raced, albeit unsuccessfully, in the 1970 Targa Florio event.

teamed by Roger Enever, Alec Poole and Clive Baker dropped out at an early stage with overheating. As it happened, this was the last occasion an official MG team competed on a European race track and, from thereon, the competitive accent was concentrated on rallying saloon cars.

Nevertheless the two special lightweights put in swansong appearances at Sebring in 1969 though they were entered by British Leyland's North American subsidiary. Both cars finished, Paddy Hopkirk and Andrew Hedges doing best in fifteenth position. And that, alas, really was the end.

Chapter 5

MG RV8 — The marque has returned

SO THAT was the end of the MGB, or was it? Twelve and a half years after the model had ceased production, on 19 April 1993 the first example of its spiritual successor, the MG RV8, left the Rover Group's purpose-built Cowley assembly line. This low volume car is only destined for a two-year manufacturing life, but on a broader canvas it heralds the rebirth of the MG name, for Rover has unequivocally proclaimed: 'The marque has returned.'

To chart the course of this extraordinary turnabout in MG's fortunes, we must retrace our steps to 1980, when the Abingdon factory was closed, and to the performance of the then BL Cars because, as ever, MG is inexorably linked to the prosperity of its corporate parent. In the same year of 1980, Triumph production also ceased at Canley, although the next car to bear the name was the Cowley-built Acclaim of 1981. This was the first fruit of a collaboration, signed in 1979, between the Japanese Honda company and BL which was a recognition by its chairman, Sir Michael Edwardes, that a joint development programme with a similar sized car company was essential if the British firm was to survive.

The demise of this Honda Ballade-based Triumph in 1984 saw that marque pass into oblivion, a move which followed the last Morris car having been built in the previous year. The Acclaim's 1.3 litre Ballade-related replacement was the Rover 200, and the smallest capacity car to be so called since 1948. This boded ill for the Austin make which disappeared in 1987, and its demise left BL with just two marque names: Rover. . . and MG. The famous octagonal badge that had, appropriately, continued to appear from 1982 on the high-performance versions of the popular and indigenous Metro, was also applied to the similarly conceived Maestro hatchback of 1983 and to its Montego saloon stablemate that arrived in 1984.

But overall, BL's vehicle profile was being tilted away from volume towards specialist production, a move that was further reinforced by the arrival, in 1986, of the top-line Rover 800 range that took over from the Solihull-designed SD1 hatchback and, similarly, perpetuated Japanese collaboration. It was available with a BL-created 2 litre M16 engine or a choice of Honda V6 units.

Sir Michael Edwardes had stepped down in 1982 and he left a greatly slimmed down, though still state-owned, car company. He was succeeded by Sir Austin Bide, but in 1986 Graham Day took over as chairman, and he promptly renamed the business the Rover Group. In 1988, it was purchased from a grateful government by British Aerospace, and the Honda association was underpinned in 1990 when it took a 20 per cent share in Rover's £520 million equity. For its part, Rover took a reciprocal 20 per cent holding in the newly created Honda UK Manufacturing. The business remains so constituted at the time of writing (1993).

After generations of inefficiently operating from multifarious factories scattered throughout the country, Rover car production is today concentrated on two well equipped plants at Cowley and Longbridge, while Defender, Discovery and Range Rover manufacture continues at Solihull, car-making having been transferred to the former facility in 1981. The industrial anarchy which once plagued the company is now a thing of the past, and in 1992, despite making a £49 million loss, Rover's Metro, 200/400 family, the revised 800 and four wheel drive vehicles performed relatively well at a time when the British economy was in deep recession. Such was the improvement in the firm's affairs that in May 1993 *The Daily Telegraph* heralded Rover as the 'Most Improved Car Maker of the Decade'.

Although so many of the Group's marque names have gone, they are far from forgotten. This is thanks to the confidence that Rover has shown in its British Motor Industry Heritage Trust subsidiary, whose activities culminated in May 1993 with the opening of the £8 million Heritage Motor Centre at Gaydon, Warwickshire. The Trust's origins reach back to 1975 when Alex Park, general manager of the newly nationalised Leyland Cars, approved the creation of Leyland Historic Vehicles, and in 1978 LHV, which largely consisted of Richard Westcott and Ron Whitehead, moved from Longbridge to the grounds of the BL training centre at Studley Castle, Warwickshire. In May 1979 came a change of name to BL Heritage, and Peter Mitchell, formerly senior keeper of industry and technology at the Coventry Museums, was appointed managing director. In 1980 Heritage adventurously launched an approval scheme for companies which specialised in the sale and manufacture of obsolete parts for vehicles formerly built by BL Cars' predecessors, and today there are some 50 members of the Association of Heritage Approved Specialists.

In 1983 came a change in status when BL Heritage loosened its ties with its corporate origins and was effectively replaced by the British Motor Industry Heritage Trust. This educational trust was intended to embrace all Britain's car makers, but management

British Motor Heritage executive director, David Bishop (standing right) in 1988 with the original BMH team which built the MGB bodyshells. Left to right, standing: manufacturing manager, Jack Bellinger, George Milne, Bernard Hartley-Yates. Front row: Alan Beckett, Bill Bailey.

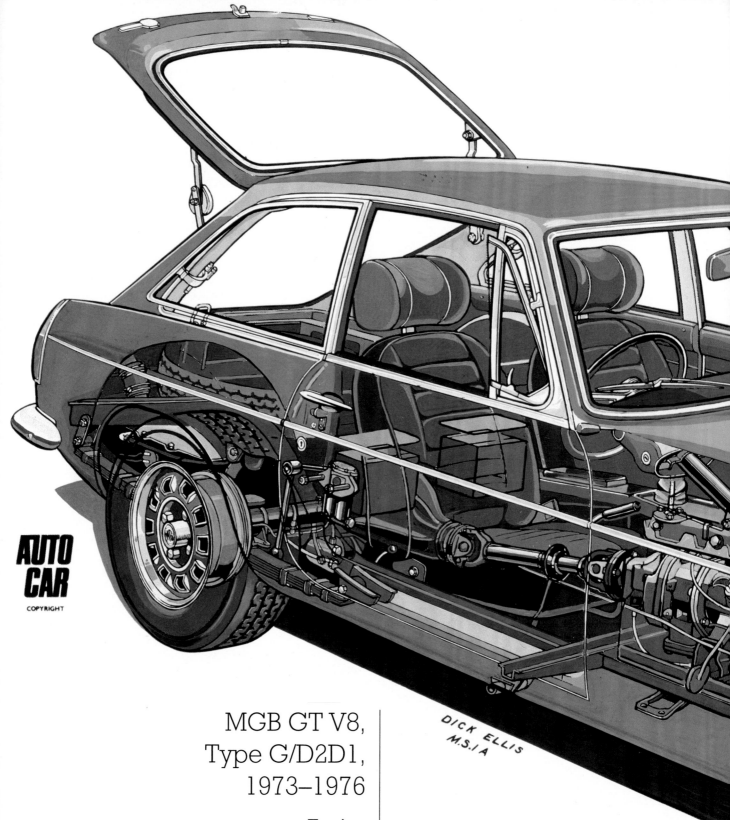

MGB GT V8,
Type G/D2D1,
1973–1976

DICK ELLIS
M.S.I A

Engine

Cylinders: 90 degree V8
Bore: 88.96 mm
Stroke: 71.1 mm
Displacement: 3528 cc
Valves: Pushrod/overhead
Compression ratio: 8.25:1
Carburettors: Twin 1.75 in SU HIF6
Power output: 137 bhp at 5000 rpm

Transmission

Clutch: Borg and Beck 9.5 in single dry-plate
diaphragm
Gearbox: 4-speed, all synchromes
Ratios: Top 1.0, 3rd 1.25, 2nd 1.97, 1st 3.13, reverse
2.81
Overdrive: Standard. Laycock LH type top 0.82
Final drive: 3.07:1

Chassis

Construction: Unitary
Brakes:Lockheed servo-assisted
Front: 10.7 in discs
Rear: 10 x 1.7 in drum
Steering: Rack and pinion, collapsible column, 2.9 turns lock to lock
Suspension – front: Coil spring, wishbone
Suspension – rear: Half elliptic, leaf spring
Wheels: Composite 5J cast alloy centres, chrome steel rims.

Dimensions & weight

Wheelbase: 7 ft 7 in
Track – front: 4 ft 1 in
Track – rear: 4 ft 1.25 in
Overall length: 12 ft 10.7 in
Overall width: 5ft
Overall height: 4 ft 2 in
Ground clearance: 4.5 in
Turning circle: 34 ft
Kerb weight: 21.6 cwt

Performance

Maximum speed: 123 mph
Acceleration: 0-60 mph 8.6 secs
Overall fuel consumption: 23 mpg

Production

Deliveries: UK, 2591. No overseas sales.

The Rover V8 engine which powers the MG RV8 has been used in the MGB before. Between 1973 and 1976, it was employed in its original 3.5 litre state in the MGB GT V8.

Two Rover executives closely involved with the MG RV8, John Towers (left), managing director of the Group with Peter Mitchell, managing director of British Motor Heritage and the British Motor Industry Heritage Trust. The occasion was the official handing over of the first production RV8, in April 1993, which is displayed at the Heritage Motor Centre at Gaydon, Warwickshire.

changes at Ford saw it withdraw from BMIHT and it was followed by Vauxhall. With the departure of the American-owned sector, the Trust reverted to its root companies which, nevertheless, represented more than 70 per cent of the country's motoring history.

Following the Trust's creation, its parts and approval scheme was hived off to a new subsidiary in the shape of the Cowley-based British Motor Heritage, of which Peter Mitchell is also managing director. This was to be the cash-generating arm of the Trust and 75 per cent of its profits are covenanted to support the activities of BMIHT. It is a unique organisation within the British motor industry in being formed to provide a service to owners of cars built by Rover, and its

predecessors, which have been out of production for more than eight years. Since 1988 British Motor Heritage has manufactured the MGB bodyshell, and it is this initiative that has played a pivotal role in the creation of the new MG RV8 and, in turn, the revival of the MG marque.

It was in 1984 that David Bishop, formerly of Pressed Steel Fisher and with 23 years of body manufacture to his credit, joined the Heritage organisation as assistant managing director. During 1986 a piece of paper landed on his desk which authorised the scrapping of the TR7 body tools which, alas, occurred, but it triggered the then audacious thought of BMH reintroducing the bodyshell of MGB, which had then been out of production for six years. Bishop spent much of the first half of 1987 tracking down the original pressing tools and jigs, which, thankfully, survived in-house at the former Pressed Steel plant at Swindon. Virtually all were recovered.

At this stage, British Motor Heritage had no manufacturing facility so a factory unit was occupied at Faringdon, Oxfordshire. Bishop says that this location was deliberately chosen because it is approximately mid-way between

Cowley and Swindon, where, amongst others, the MGB bodies had been built, and BMH could thus draw on expertise from both of these skills centres.

A key appointment came in the shape of Jack Bellinger, who was on the point of retiring but had a lifetime of experience at Pressed Steel at Cowley. He became manufacturing manager, and initially a small six-strong team was recruited. The project had been given the green light in the autumn of 1987 and the first body was completed on 20 February 1988. As mentioned on page 145, the bodyshell was launched in April of that year. This was the pre-1975 chrome-bumpered right hand drive roadster and it was joined by its American specification equivalent in 1990. A short run of MBG GTs was built and the right hand drive rubber-bumpered roadster of 1975/80 vintage followed in 1991. With the success of the MGB project, BMH wasted little time in also reintroducing the MG Midget shell, of which 500 have been made, and this was followed in 1992 by the TR6 hull that has so far found 100 customers.

The scheme has therefore proved to be a resounding success. Five years on, David Bishop, who became an executive director of BMH in 1988, reflects that, 'with hindsight, it looks so easy but at the time no one had done anything similar. We thought that the market might stand 250 to 300 shells, but we've now built around 3,000.'

Soon after the MGB bodyshell's 1988 launch, Bishop accepted an invitation from Colin Dryden, motoring correspondent on *The Sunday Telegraph*, to address a lunchtime meeting of the Fleet Street Motoring Group, of which he was chairman, at Duffers, a pub near to London's Ludgate Circus. The subject of Bishop's talk was, naturally, the MGB bodyshell. 'But at the end of it, as journalists do, everyone said, "What next? You've done the hardest bit. What about building a car?" I fielded them off but as we came away John Brigden, who handles our public relations, said to me, "You've got to look at that seriously." And I did.'

Stephen Schlemmer (left), director of the Gaydon-based Rover Special Products and MG RV8 project director, Graham Irvine, located at Cowley, pictured with the first production RV8 at Cowley.

The MG RV8 pictured against the magnificent scenery of the Cambrian Mountains in mid Wales.

MGB
The illustrated history

British Motor Heritage had, in fact, already built one MGB when the shell had been launched at *Classic Cars'* National Classic Motor Show at the Birmingham National Exhibition Centre in April. Registered TAX 192G, it has been retained by BMH and is still affectionately known as 'Taxi'. However, Bishop was in no doubt that any revived MGB should be powered by the Rover V8 engine used in the MGB GT V8 model, built between 1973 and 1976.

Having said that, the MGB was best known in its four-cylinder form, and to satisfy himself of the practicality or otherwise of producing such a version, he initiated a feasibility study to discover how easily the B bodyshell would accept Rover's twin overhead camshaft M16 four, and there was soon little doubt that it required extensive surgery to accommodate the engine. To consolidate his findings, in mid 1988 Bishop borrowed from Morgan a Plus 4 which had just been reintroduced with the M16 unit, and he then drove it from Malvern to Baldock, Hertfordshire and to the premises of the MG Specialists Brown and Gammons. 'I much value Ron Gammons' judgement and I borrowed his MGB GT V8 for comparative purposes. Ron then drove both cars and we decided that the two were poles apart. The four just didn't have the tautness of the V8.' There was a further overwhelming advantage, because all the post–1974 model year B bodyshells had already been tailored to accept the light alloy eight, regardless of whether it was being fitted or not.

When current, the MGB GT V8 had, of course, been a closed car because in its day the rubber-bumpered roadster had lacked the torsional rigidity of the GT. Yet Bishop was convinced that if revived the MG could be produced in touring form because the hand-built BMH shell was not made under a piece-work system, has more spot welds than the original and is therefore considerably stronger. He was also the first to recognise that 'there was no beating an open-topped sports car'.

Next, he discussed the feasibility of the project with Peter Mitchell, managing director

Top: Building the MG RV8 body at the British Motor Heritage's factory at Pioneer Road, Faringdon, Oxfordshire. Here the luggage floor is being welded to the boot assembly.

Middle: The gearbox drive shaft tunnel going together, prior to its attachment to the front end.

Bottom: Front end assembly, with inner wing arches and bonnet slam panel in place. The exhaust pipe aperture can be seen in the centre foreground.

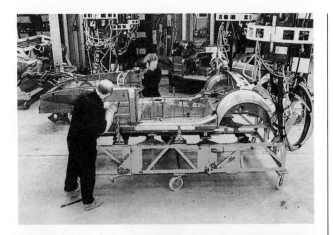

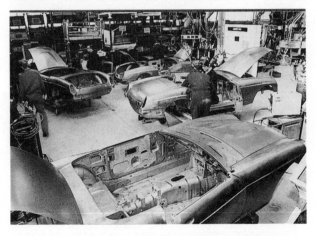

Top: The front and rear assembly comes together on the main frame station.

Middle: The body is then inverted in this jig for underbody welding.

Bottom: Four MG RV8 bodies, now with their doors, bonnets and boot lids nearing completion.

of British Motor Heritage. It should be made clear that Bishop was not envisaging a car of the type that emerged as the RV8. What he had in mind was a V8-engined version of the MGB roadster, with some enhancement to its interior trim.

'Peter didn't need much convincing because he thought that it was a good idea!' But Bishop got a rather different response from BMIHT's chairman, Les Wharton, who was also, significantly, managing director of Austin Rover. 'He is a dour Lancastrian whose commercial judgement I respect enormously and he was adamant when he told me, "The last thing you want to do within Heritage is to build a complete car. You haven't got the wherewithal or the facilities." He could, nevertheless, see the attraction of the idea because it would have meant an instant sale for the bodyshells we were producing.' Despite Wharton's reservations, Bishop 'kept pestering away' within the higher echelons of Rover. 'The market was still there and we really did need to go for it.'

In the meantime, BMH had produced its left hand drive chrome-bumpered version of the MGB for the American market and, perhaps even more significantly, Rover had decided to reintroduce the Mini Cooper, which had ceased production in 1971. It had the advantage of employing a current bodyshell but was a distinguished contemporary of the MGB. . .

There the matter rested until early in 1990 and a large/medium car planning meeting, held at Canley and chaired by John Towers, then the Rover Group's product development director. Bishop had been asked to make a presentation of the V8-engined MGB and to do so he borrowed from an enthusiast an MGB roadster that had been so converted and which 'whistled like an orchestra'. It was joined by BMH's faithful Open B 'Taxi', and a Morgan Plus 8, which used the Rover V8 engine. The meeting bore fruit. Bishop recalls that they 'were sold then and there on an MGB V8' and British Motor Heritage was given a brief to 'build a car'.

This was undertaken in some secrecy by Heritage mechanic Mark Gamble, who usually worked at Studley, and already had experience of constructing, amongst other cars, the Classic Car Show MGB. He lives at Bromsgrove and the car was built in the Heritage storage facility in the village of Snitterfield, near Stratford on Avon. It was also conveniently close to Bishop's own home and he could therefore keep an eye on the project.

Mark began work in March 1990, the job took approximately three months to execute

MG RV8, 1993-1995

Engine
Cylinders: 90 degree V8
Bore: 94 mm
Stroke: 71 mm
Displacement: 3946 cc
Valves: Pushrod/overhead
Compression ratio: 9.35:1
Fuel injection: Lucas multi point injection
Power output: 190 PS at 4750 rpm

Transmission
Gearbox: 5-speed LT 77, all synchromesh
Ratios: Top 0.79, 4th 1.00, 3rd 1.40, 1st 3.32
Final drive: 3.31:1

Chassis
Construction: Unitary
Brakes: Lockheed vacuum servo assisted
Front: 270 mm ventilated discs
Rear: 280 mm drums
Steering: Rack and pinion
Suspension – front: Double wishbone and coil
sprint, dampers, anti-roll bar
Suspension – rear: Twin taper leaf half elliptic
spring,s dampers, control arms, anti-roll bar
Wheels: Cast alloy 15 in x 6J

Dimensions & weight
Wheelbase: 7 ft 8 in
Track – front: 4ft 1in
Track – rear: 4 ft 4 in
Overall length: 13 ft 2 in
Overall width: 5 ft 7 in
Overall height: 4 ft 4 in
Kerb weight: 25.2 cwt

Performance
Maximum speed: 135 mph
Acceleration: 0-60 mph 6.9 secs
Overall fuel consumption: 20.2 mpg

Production
Deliveries: UK, 324; Overseas, 1,672; total 1,996

and was finished in May. The conversion was carried out in a workshop, with its windows blacked over to exclude prying eyes, and the donor car was a white, left hand drive, rubber-bumpered MGB roadster, registered LFC 436S. Its four-cylinder engine was removed and replaced with a 3.5 litre V8 that Bishop has already secured from Rover's Power Train division at Solihull. The mountings were fabricated at Faringdon, but despite the unit being positioned as low as possible, the Lucas LE electronic fuel injection system was still well proud of the bonnet.

Gamble recalls, 'We cut a hole in it and covered it with a biscuit tin!' The gearbox was Rover's '77 mm' manual gearbox and its fitment required some modifications to the transmission tunnel because it is much taller than the original. Drive was taken via a rare limited slip differential contained within one of the equally scarce MGB GT V8 rear axles. The original Rostyle wheels were retained.

Great attention was paid to the suspension, which was stiffened up in the manner employed on competition Bs. Similarly, the braking was uprated and the front discs replaced by the more robust Range Rover units and callipers. New parts came from Heritage-approved suppliers and some second-hand ones were also needed. There were the obligatory two seats, but trim was otherwise virtually non-existent, and at the request of Rover the car was sprayed Flame Red. Once the work was finished, Mark took the V8-powered B on a 1,200 mile weekend trip to Cornwall. 'I suppose that it must have been capable of around 130 mph and it went very well. It was extremely tractable and really came into its own on motorways.' This trip produced no major problems and the B was then taken over by David Bishop.

He continued to run the car in the following week and reported a few insignificant peccadillos. As proven components were being used, reliability was not a problem, but Bishop, who readily acknowledges that the car was 'horrendously rough', was anxious for a professional chassis engineer to appraise the handling of the V8-

The finished BMH built shell, ready for delivery to Cowley.

powered MGB. Since 1979, when it became fully operational, BL Cars and its Rover Group successor have greatly benefited from a much-needed test and research facility located on a former Strike Command and V bomber airfield at Gaydon, Warwickshire, which is within easy reach of the industrial Midlands.

It was there that David Bishop entrusted the B, by then shod with the V8's alloy wheels, to chassis engineer Rob Oldaker for evaluation. Bishop recalls him taking the MG 'around the service road. I was following in a Vitesse [800] and was left behind!' After the run, Oldaker told Bishop that, in his view, the B was 'not yet right but it's a project and something that we can refine'. After being

returned to Heritage, the car was later handed over to Rover's newly established Special Products division which is also based at Gaydon.

Until 1990, Rover's priority had been to get its mainstream product range right. By then its agreement with Honda was running smoothly and the association was further consolidated in 1991 to reach into the twenty-first century. The liaison has proved to be of mutual benefit to both parties; collaboration has helped Rover to develop a cost-effective and successful family of cars, while in 1992 Honda, opened on a manufacturing plant at Swindon from which it could produce models for the British and European market.

But from Rover's standpoint, while the company was progressively to create a distinctive 'Rover identity' for its later cars, it began to recognise that it was in its interests to produce some vehicles which could be seen as being demonstrably different from those of its Japanese associate: what is describes as 'niche cars'. In 1992, the Group's chairman George Simpson, told *Autocar & Motor* that: 'As long as Rover continues to work with Honda, low volume, specialist cars will be on the price lists. "We need niche cars more than ever now. . . to keep the image up and to differentiate our cars from Honda's."

On one hand, this meant such projects as the 800 coupe and a cabriolet version of the 200 and, on the other, cars like the Mini Cooper and. . . MG RV8. When David Bishop had been first trying to convince Rover executives of the appeal of a V8-engined MGB, he found that 'they liked the idea but could not see how it fitted within the company'. The development of the niche car

The open road beckons; the RV8's beautifully appointed interior is shown to good effect. The Welsh location was chosen by Rover for its official photographs of the MG as it fulfilled the dual requirements of beautiful but remote scenery and thus security, the car not having been officially released when they were taken.

The Cowley build team with the first production MG RV8. Manufacturing manager, Cliff Law, is on the extreme left.

philosophy answered that question and this is where Rover's Special Products division comes in.

Since its creation in January 1990, RSP has been under the direction of Stephen Schlemmer, an engineer who began his career with Perkins diesel engines and joined what was Leyland Cars in 1977. He has worked in business and planning ever since and was product planning manager on the highly successful Austin Metro of 1980. His involvement with the MG name stems from the development of the Metro's popular derivative. In the mid 1980s, Schlemmer moved to Land Rover, where he was new projects director, and he provides the background for the divisions's creation.

'The Rover board set up RSP for niche product opportunities to explore areas of the market that the company was not covering. At one end, Land Rover had an operation for one-off conversions and there were volume cars at the other, but nothing in between. We were to look at gaps in the range and to explore the image end of the market and carefully target the customer.'

As far as the public was concerned, the first occupant of a Rover 'niche', announced in July 1990, was the limited edition of the Mini

Cooper, confined to 1,000 cars, as a prelude to the model's reintroduction in September. That month came an exclusive version of the old-style Range Rover, the CSK – which are the initials of its creator, Charles Spencer King – that was restricted to a mere 200 vehicles. Other projects have included a similarly targeted American version of the newly introduced Land Rover Defender and the Mini and Metro cabriolets. All these exercises were undertaken on existing vehicles but the MG RV8 project has necessitated considerably more work, because although based on the MGB substructure, it has involved the creation of a new model, but one with its origins firmly rooted in the best-selling sports car.

'The idea of the MG RV8 was largely driven by the fact that Heritage had reintroduced the bodyshell but it was not in business to make new cars. There was also further input from within the company.'

First, RSP had to satisfy itself that there was a market for an MGB-based car. Relying as it did on the relatively limited output of the

225

Left: An RV8 in the final stages of build at the MG Low Volume Assembly facility at Cowley. In the background are Rover managing director, John Towers (left) and project director Graham Irvine.

Faringdon-built hull, any vehicle that resulted would, by its nature, be a low production exercise. In April 1991, the RSP team began to undertake a demographic study which, in effect, asked the public, 'What does MG mean to you, what does Rover mean, what does sporting motoring mean?'

Schlemmer says, 'In fact we got a very good reaction. People saw MG as a marque with positive attributes, although it was as if it were in suspension. Most knew that Rover owned MG and saw it as something on the shelf, but one which could be taken down and dusted off.'

The customer body identified by RSP as potential purchasers of the car would be successful people who already owned a number of vehicles, including an executive saloon, but found them boring. 'They might have had an MG in the past or, on the other hand, recalled the pleasures of open air motoring, even though they might never have experienced them!'

Special Products also 'needed to know that MG would work within Rover and that there would be a story behind it'. As the MGB had been introduced at the 1962 Motor Show, the autumn of 1992 would therefore be the thirtieth anniversary of its announcement. This provided the perfect 'hook' on which to hang the model, and in turn meant a projected launch at the 1992 Motor Show.

Having said that, there was no question of the B being reintroduced in its original form. Schlemmer explains: 'What we decided to do was to create a car which would have been the top of the range model, if the MGB had not gone out of production.'

By June of 1991, RSP was in a position to put a proposition to the Rover board. 'To an outsider, this might sound a rather cold and heartless proposal which set down how much the car was going to cost us to make and how long it would take to pay us back. But our programmes work because they are of short duration and cost effective.' The proposal was accompanied with a model of the proposed MG; the outcome was a directorial green light and RSP was told to 'go away and do it'.

As will have become apparent, the MG RV8 is a low volume model aimed at a very different clientele to the original car and, says Schlemmer, 'we are going to build them at 15

Making a splash: an MG RV8 head on. Headlamps are courtesy of the Porsche 911.

MGB
The illustrated history

a week for a couple of years. There is no question of us going beyond the 2,000 figure.'

Rover Special Products consists of director Stephen Schlemmer and a 30-strong engineering team, of which 12 were allocated to the RV8 project. However, in developing the MG RV8, RSP was also able to draw on the resources of the entire Rover Group and the number of individuals involved therefore runs into hundreds. It has also recruited the services of outside agencies: 'We take ideas from lots of people, put them together and make them work.'

The RV8's lines shown to good effect. This example, finished in the optional colour of Le Mans Green, is prototype ADDVAL07, which was externally identical to the finished car although its engine compartment differed somewhat from the production version.

Any project requires a codename, and in the case of the MG it was Adder. This came about because, recalls Schlemmer, 'Early on one or two people said, "This V8-engined MG is the English AC Cobra." And the nearest thing to an English cobra is an adder.'

The body changes envisaged were first executed on the Heritage-built development car which, accordingly, became unrecognisable, it also having been converted to right hand drive and resprayed green. It had been joined by a second, Snitterfield-built development vehicle titled DEV 2, again the work of Mark Gamble, which was built up around an original and unused right hand drive rubber-bumpered MGB roadster bodyshell, BMH not having yet built its own. Also sprayed Flame Red, it was registered YWU 486S and as what had become DEV 1 was being used for styling work, its precious limited slip differential was transferred to the second development car. Similarly, the bonnet of the first V8-powered B, complete with its obligatory biscuit tin, was also fitted. On arrival at Gaydon, DEV 2 was soon being used as a hardworking mule, later the 3.9 litre V8 was fitted and it became test bed for

evaluating engine cooling. Externally, DEV 2 remained an MGB roadster and was to be joined by a handful of Gaydon-built Validation Vehicles.

It is wholly in the traditions of the marque that in developing an MG model, Rover, as its corporate parent, should dig deeply into its parts bin and the vast majority of the RV8's components come from that source. The company has also drawn on those of other manufacturers and the MG has Porsche 911 headlamps, the arm rest is from a 'major volume manufacturer' and there are a few Jaguar components. The outcome is a vehicle which consists of about five per cent of MGB parts, 20 per cent are improved, retooled, resourced MGB while the 75 per cent balance is new to the B.

The car is, in overall terms, slightly longer and also wider than the B, and its wheelbase, at 7 ft 8 in, is an inch greater. While its appearance is chunky, purposeful and distinctive, it still retains the unflickering spirit of the original and it is, not surprisingly, faster. In 1973, *Autocar* credited the 3.5 litre MGB GT V8 – which was, of course, a closed car – with a top speed of 123.9 mph and with

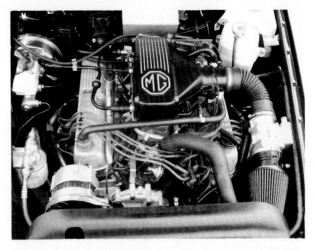

The 3.9 litre Rover V8 engine, as installed in the RV8. The purpose designed MG plenum chamber is fitted at Cowley.

being able to reach 60 mph in 8.6 seconds. The RV8, with its larger 3.9 litre engine, is approximately 2 cwt heavier than the GT, at 25.2 cwt, and Rover claim that it is a 135 mph car with 60 mph coming up from standstill in 5.9 seconds.

The basis of the RV8 is the Heritage-built MGB underframe, 'the solid, bombproof structure is still there' says Schlemmer. The doors have been retained, less their quarterlights, the remainder of the body panels are new. Both front and rear wings are flared to accommodate the cast alloy 15 x 6J wheels which are shod with 205/65 x 15VR radial ply tyres. Extensive use is made of single and double-sided, zinc-plated steels and the car carries a six-year anti-corrosion warranty. The bumpers echo the body colours, and the front ones incorporate indicator and fog lamps, whilst there is no radiator grille as such, but a false honeycomb which conceals the radiator proper.

And there is a new badge. When the MGA was discontinued in 1962, it still bore the traditional combination of a chocolate MG monogram set against a cream octagonal background, introduced at the 1927 Motor Show. The A's MGB replacement bore a new badge, with chrome lettering and a red background, which was used throughout the model's production life and, latterly, had been applied to Rover's MG saloons which had been discontinued in 1991. But Schlemmer felt that the RV8 deserved something new and the renowned octagon has been subtly recreated and reverted to the chocolate and cream hues of the 1927/62 era. The badge appears on the car's bonnet, boot lid and the wheel

centres, where it plays a security role, and can only be removed by application of an appropriate Allen key.

Under the bonnet is the derivative of the aluminium alloy V8 which powered the original MG V8 and is the same fuel-injected unit that Rover supplies to Morgan for its Plus 8 and TVR's Griffith and Chimaera, although the RV8 has its own plenum chamber bearing the MG octagon. The 3.5 litre twin SU carburettored unit originally employed on its MG predecessor developed 137 bhp at 5,000 rpm, while the present day V8, enlarged to 3.9 litres in 1990, has 187 bhp on tap. Current refinements include an engine management system controlling fuel injection, ignition and engine diagnostics. Control of the three-way closed loop catalysts is via feedback from Lambda sensors located in the exhaust manifolds. The V8 runs on unleaded fuel.

Quite intentionally, the engine bay also *looks* impressive. Schlemmer says, 'We put a lot of effort into the underbonnet appearance, hence the new cast aluminium manifold. We've made the engine compartment very tidy because, I think, people want to lift the bonnet.'

A stainless steel twin pipe exhaust system is fitted and this, once again, reflects the thought that has gone into the project. 'One of the things that I wanted to do at Land Rover was to get a proper divided V8 exhaust system on the Range Rover. I therefore insisted that on the MG the pipes be separate, although they actually go through the same silencer in two places, and there are twin pipes at the back, all of which contributes to a proper V8 burble.'

The five-speed gearbox, built by Land Rover, is the current version of the company's '77 mm' gearbox, introduced in 1976, and so called because that is the distance between the centre lines of the main shaft and lay shaft. Drive goes to a live rear axle, which has a Quaife torque bias differential to cope with the power developed by the V8. It constantly redistributes torque to the wheel with the most traction.

Great attention has been paid to the suspension and RSP engineers studied the

Main picture: The RV8, which sells for £25,440, with an appropriately opulent clientele.

Inset: The RV8's magnificent interior which is upholstered in Stone Beige coloured leather and Elm burr wood veneer is used to good effect on the fascia and door cappings.

efforts made at stiffening it up by enthusiasts who race MGBs. Some changes have also been made to the front suspension. 'We wanted to update the original integral lever arms dampers' and these have been replaced by more conventional double wishbones with coil springs and concentric tubular dampers which have necessitated modifications to the front cross member. This came about because 'we had an engineer on the team who happened to design single-seater racing and hill climb cars. He had done some work for the aftermarket on coil springs and telescopic damper suspension and he was able to build on that.'

The geometry is, however, virtually identical to the original, whilst detail changes have been made to the bushing and bearings. The rack and pinion steering is a mildly modified MGB component. At the rear, the half elliptic springs are perpetuated although the multileaves have been replaced by twin taper single leaf ones and there are two lower torque control arms.

In layout, the servo braking system reflects that of the MGB and was developed with the racing division of Automotive Products. It is uprated with 270 mm diameter ventilated discs and four piston callipers at the front and the 230 mm rear drums are similar to the originals.

As far as the RV8's interior is concerned, Schlemmer explains that: 'to support the price, it had to have a stunning appearance. The sort of people at which the car is aimed would want a very high level of comfort and opulence, particularly as this is a straightforward car, with no electric windows, hood, power steering or automatic 'box. They like the idea of a classic car but it would need to be comfortable enough so they could, if they wished, jump into it and drive, say, to the Lake District for the weekend.'

The car is therefore upholstered in Stone Beige Connolly leather, and the material extends to the head restraints, the MG

monogrammed steering wheel and door-mounted arm rests. The general feeling of well-being is complemented by Dark Stone Beige carpeting.

This quality approach is extended to the fascia which is finished in Elm Burr wood veneer, and is also applied to the centre console and door cappings. It has the additional virtue of showing off the circular, black-faced instruments to good effect. There is a new hood, by Tickford, and a single-piece windscreen replaces the original.

The standard body colours are shared with the 600/800 Rover saloon range, and the MG is available in Flame Red, British Racing Green, Black, Caribbean Blue, White Gold and Nightfire Red. A further four special colours are unique to the RV8, which are Oxford Blue, Woodcote Green, Old English White and Le Mans Green.

Schlemmer has also incorporated an idea, proffered by the MG Car Club, of reviving the Abingdon tradition of the beginning an MG's chassis number with 251, which was the factory telephone number. The practice had ceased in 1954 but has been revived in 1993 for the RV8, although today's cars have a multi-digited VIN, or Vehicle Identification Number.

When it came to naming the MG, 'We

Rear view of the RV8 with its hood lowered. Unlike the MGB, there is no external door handle to the boot; it is electrically released from the cockpit. But like the B, the MG badge is retained. Fog warning lamps are contained within the rear bumper.

looked at all the letters of the alphabet and they had all been used at one time or another. We chose R because it sounded right, but it doesn't actually stand for anything and is whatever you want it to be: Rover, Reintroduction or Rebirth. . .'

The RV8 is only being built in right hand drive form and will therefore be sold almost exclusively on the British market. As for other areas, Schlemmer says that Rover might be looking for some right hand drive sales in Europe but these would be in penny numbers 'or tens and twenties'. RSP is also 'very seriously' considering 'a few hundred cars' for Japan, a country which also drives on the left. That would necessitate the fitment of an air conditioning system, but the interest that the MG has generated there might justify it.

By January 1992 the car's external appearance had been finalised, so that month the RV8 was unveiled to a wider – though still in-house – audience at a Rover dealers' convention, held at Birmingham's National

The MG with its Tickford hood raised. It is only available in black and a zip down rear window is fitted. Note that the RV8 lacks the quarter lights of the MGB.

Indoor Arena. At one of the presentations, where the MG was the last car to be unveiled, the assembled multitude rose to its collective feet and clapped. . .

During 1992, Rover's public affairs department began to feed the motoring press with a carefully orchestrated dribble of 'teasers' relating to the RV8. Most significantly, in June came the first official photograph which tantalisingly showed a side view that achieved its dual objective of generating considerable interest without giving away the model's new front end or its luxurious interior.

While the car's development was proceeding apace, the summer of 1992 saw its purpose-designed assembly facility nearing completion. This is located at Cowley, or what Schlemmer likes to call 'Abingdon North'. When Rover was deciding which plant it was going to use to assemble the RV8, Longbridge was ruled out because it had no spare capacity. This meant that the car could be produced at either Cowley or Solihull.

'There wasn't much to choose between them,' says Schlemmer, 'but Solihull was excluded because it would have meant transporting the bodyshells some 70 miles from Faringdon to the Midlands.' Such an exercise would have had echoes of the 1960s when MGB bodies were built at Swindon and

uneconomically delivered to Coventry. There they were painted and trimmed and then returned to Abingdon, close to where they had been made, for final assembly.

So Cowley, which is a mere 15 miles from Faringdon, was chosen and this also gave RSP access to its prototype and experimental workshop and the methods bay in S block at the South Works which was used to build more development mules, albeit for a brief period. This was because in 1990, the Rover Group had launched a two-year £200 million investment programme to consolidate its Cowley production facilities. It involved the demolition of the old Morris Motors' North and South Works, and that site is being redeveloped by Arlington Securities, a British Aerospace subsidiary, as a business and science park.

Manufacturing is therefore concentrated on a single 122 acre site on the opposite side of Oxford's Eastern Bypass at the former Body Plant, previously occupied by Pressed Steel. On its completion in 1992, Rover could justly claim this Large Car manufacturing plant to be

Sisters under the skin: the RV8 is only slightly
longer and wider than the MGB and both use
essentially the same substructure. The
simplicity of the MGB's interior, compared
with that of the RV8, is readily apparent.

one of the most advanced in Europe and
Cowley's productive capacity has more than
doubled, from 50,000 to 110,000 cars per
annum.

The workforce was encouraged to
contribute to the design of the new assembly

facilities, a dialogue which culminated in 1992
in Rover signing a Japanese-style agreement
with its employees, who now operate in teams
and take responsibility for many of their own
tasks but no longer clock in.

All these developments could only prove
to be of great benefit to Adder, and with
Cowley moving centre stage in the car's
evolution, in January 1992 the project's
manufacturing manager, Cliff Law, was
appointed to his post. His first assignment was
'to find somewhere on the site to assemble the

of the Low Volume Assembly unit we have today'.

Having got his shopping list, Law began to track down equipment made redundant by the ongoing demolition of the North and South Works. 'I said, "Is that being used, is that spare, can I have that?" There was a lot of interest in the MG project and I was able to assemble much of what we needed.' Some money was spent on metalwork and slings, hitherto used on the 800, were adapted for the MG. But the vast majority of the manufacturing equipment came from within the plant.

Law was simultaneously assembling his build team of eight though this was later expanded to 14. It would have been too easy to go out and only use former MGB workers. 'We have some but I wanted a mixture of ages and abilities.' Other members of the team come from the prototype workshop and the 800 assembly line. 'They're of mixed ages, personalities and previous experiences. We've broken down a lot of barriers in terms of what people are prepared to do. We all have our cups of tea together and there are no demarcations. They also keep the facility clean, and I sweep the floor as well!' One of the team's initiatives was to track down a supply of redundant carpet tiles which were then laid, complete with the MG monogram, in the rest room.

Although work on developing the build facility would go on throughout 1992, by July, the basic essentials were in place. This was to prove to be a great asset to Graham Irvine who, on 1 August, took over as Adder's Project Director. It meant that the all-important prototypes could, unusually, be produced on the same build facility and by the same team as the finished product. Any problems that, inevitably, arose could therefore be speedily and efficiently resolved. This was particularly important because the model's announcement was scheduled for that year's Motor Show, with the car needing to go into production as soon as possible after that.

Irvine had joined what was Leyland Cars as a graduate in 1976, and prior to his recruitment to Adder his brief had included managing Rover's prototype engineering department at Canley, and, at the beginning of 1990, moving to Cowley as part of the management team of what was coded R17 and the world now knows as the revised and very successful Rover 800 saloon range, which appeared at the end of 1991. He was responsible for prototype building and

MG and I was fortunate to locate a building that had previously been used as a body-in-white panel store'. Law then began to 'talk to people who built the MGB at Abingdon to find how the car had been assembled there'. Armed with this and other related information, in February of that year, he jotted down a rudimentary 'fag packet sketch' of the type of layout that would be required to produce the RV8 at 15 cars a week. He then 'went to see our facilities design people, they also talked to the experts, and came up with the essentials

development for which he 'used the resources of the Cowley site and the facilities at Gaydon. It was the first time we got into real team work.'

Next Irvine took over as chief engineer of the Rover 800 coupe project where he 'delivered engineering to time, to cost and to quality'. Once again, the creation of a team was a key ingredient of the task and he was to apply its disciplines and some of the personnel when he took over Adder. He is, consequently, emphatic that 'this is not the Graham Irvine Show. It is very much a team effort.'

A programme for the RV8 was laid down, in August 1992, and envisaged five phases of build, sometimes of two or three cars, occasionally as many as seven. Phase Five would be followed by volume, if 15 cars a week can be so called, and Job One was scheduled for the first week of April 1993, just eight months away.

By August, much of the work on the RV8 had been completed by Rover Special Products, 'but we were getting to the point where we required a high level of plant involvement and we needed more engineers to undertake this. Having said that, the 12-strong RSP team perpetuated its involvement with the car, a process that would continue into the first few months of volume production.

The project team that Graham Irvine assembled for Adder was drawn from throughout Rover and included engineers from the Large Car Business Unit at Cowley, Body and Pressings at Swindon, Group Engineering, which encompassed experts in the fields of design and development and purchasing. They were housed in two Portakabins conveniently located near to the build facility and, at one point, peaked at about 60 people.

Irvine went to great lengths to ensure that from the start the team worked in harmony. 'The process had to be seamless. We achieved it by making sure that the processes were fully understood, everyone was able to contribute, regardless of which plant they came from.' The Adder project differed from its predecessors in that 'the design and

development engineers would take the vehicle all the way through to production. On the Rover 200 and, to some extent, the 800, engineers did the design and then a different group of people would ensure that it was OK for manufacture.'

While this work was proceeding, the Adder was undergoing road testing and evaluation. Although the car had been previewed in the press in June 1992, the prototypes were disguised, which continued until October when the RV8 was launched at the Motor Show. There were, in all, 37 Adder prototype and test vehicles, details of which

Below: A rendering by Rover's design team of an updated MGB, following the 1988 launch of the MGB bodyshell but prior to the setting up of the Rover Special Products in 1990. The frontal treatment is strikingly similar to that of the finished car.

Bottom: The MGB theme, as updated by Rover Special Products, after identifying its target customers. It has a different radiator grille to that of the Rover design but with more elongated wheel arches which were to feature on the RV8.

can be found in Appendix Two on page 249.

A considerable amount of development work was undertaken on British motorways and the facilities at Gaydon were employed to good effect. As the RV8 is being sold almost exclusively on the UK market, testing abroad was confined to Europe; hot weather running in the South of France, sustained fast driving on the German *Autobahn* and cold weather exposure in the snows of Scandinavia.

In the meantime, the build team was not only acquainting itself with the car but also contributing ideas to improving the production process. 'They have a great sense of pride in the product and the MG name, and were encouraged to make the manufacturing side user-friendly,' says Irvine. 'The Low Volume Assembly facility differs from the usual mass production line, where an operator might have as little as three minutes to complete his work. Here he has got up to two and a half hours, and is involved with much more of the car.'

As time was of the essence, Irvine broke new ground in there only being 'one week or two between the build phases. On a large project, these can be separated by weeks or even months.' But what he describes as 'a quality maturation process' was achieved by the introduction of a Japanese technique which was already becoming established in the development of Rover's mainstream cars. Called *geba kai*, it means a form of meeting, and is intended to cut through the time-consuming bureaucracy normally associated with developing a product. Rather than calling in an individual supplier to resolve a specific problem, 'you completely bypass that. You build maybe the first or second car of the phase, bring in every major critical supplier *and* our own manufacturing and all other plant and facilities people, together with the purchasing department. This can involve anything up to 200 individuals. You can then discuss the problems of the car or cars in question and the objective is to get a rapid solution that is signed off at the time.' The improved parts are delivered in the following week and the next vehicle in the phase is therefore different and better than its predecessor.

The outcome of this approach was that the vast majority of problems associated with the Adder project were resolved early in the RV8's development. 'Looked at in terms of a curve, they should, ideally, peak at the start of the project, in this case at Phase One, and

disappear as you go into volume. With the MG, the curve was at its highest in the earliest phases of build and then fell away. Traditionally it hadn't happened that way! What had occurred throughout the industry was that the curve was sometimes at its height just prior to the start of volume and then everyone started to panic. . . And that doesn't do the vehicle or the people involved with it any good.'

The Cowley development programme was continuing apace when, just before the MG's Motor Show debut, the car was shown to 40 representatives of the MG Car and Owners' Clubs. Stephen Schlemmer remembers: 'We'd done a similar exercise with the MG Metro and we waited, with baited breath, for their reaction. But when they saw the RV8 they were over the moon.'

The launch proper was at the Show, held at Birmingham's National Exhibition Centre, which opened on 20 October. While Rover's stand was packed with new cars, *Autocar & Motor* reported that '. . . the MG was the centre of attention. . . Rover says the levels of interest in the car exceed any it has ever seen – more than 2,000 information packs had gone on the opening morning alone'. Around 1,000 serious enquiries turned into over 200 deposits of £2,500 which accounted for the first four months of production.

The RV8's price was set at £25,440 and it thus shares a similar market sector to the even more traditional Rover V8-powered Morgan Plus 8, at £24,821, while the current glass fibre-bodied, and also V8-engined, TVR Chimaera retails for £26,250.

Back at Cowley, the project was reaching its final stages; the Phase Five cars were extremely close to the finished product and were dispatched to Rover dealers for sales demonstration purposes. On 30 March 1993, the first RV8, VIN no. SARRAWBMBMG000251 and destined for the Heritage Motor Centre at Gaydon, left the Cowley assembly line. The first six customer cars were completed two weeks later, on 19 April. 'We missed our target date by two weeks,' says Irvine. 'It would have been great to say that we hit Job One on time, but test work lags behind build so we were delayed for the right reasons.'

Each RV8 takes 19 man-hours to build and the bodies arrive from the Cowley paintshop, having begun life at the British Motor Heritage plant at nearby Faringdon which has made the transition from building the MGB bodyshell for the enthusiast market.

Not only does it now occupy three factory units, but also the workforce has risen from the original six in 1987 to 30, of which 12 are employed on the RV8 shells. The others are kept busy on the production of the original MG and Triumph bodies for which there is an ongoing demand.

As the basis of the RV8 body is the MGB underframe, in November 1991, BMH began to produce, for the first time, rubber-bumpered right hand drive hulls. This was not because of a sudden demand for them but for the team to familiarise itself with the shell which was to form the substructure of the RV8.

In 1992 came the next stage, as Heritage began pilot runs of the body proper, with wings supplied by Abbey Panels of Coventry while Rover Body and Pressings at Swindon makes the doors, bonnet and boot lid panels, just as it did for the MGB in its Pressed Steel days. The majority of the smaller parts are tooled and pressed at Faringdon. At the time of my visit in May 1993, output of these hand-assembled and spot-welded bodies was running at the projected rate of 15 a week and

there is a resident Rover inspector who meticulously examines every shell. He marks the slightest imperfection which is then rectified on the spot.

Each takes 27 man-hours to complete and up to eight bodies-in-white are then conveyed, in BMH's Leyland DAF transporter, twice a week to the Rover Group's Cowley works. There the first stop is the paint shop where they undergo an identical treatment to the 600 and 800 Rover saloons that are built at the plant. Those RV8s on which customers have specified special paintwork take a little longer.

The painted bodies are then moved on to the Low Volume Assembly facility which is about the size of two tennis courts. On arrival, the shells are injected with an anti-corrosive

In 1988 British Motor Heritage celebrated the arrival of the MGB bodyshell by commissioning this symbolic illustration of the model's renaissance which, prophetically, would lead in 1993 to the arrival of the MG RV8.

wax, and once this has been undertaken the build process can begin. It starts with fitting such items as the wiring harness and heater, petrol tank, rear axle and front suspension. The engines arrive from Solihull, just as they might at Morgan or TVR, but at Cowley the V8's plenum chamber is removed and replaced with a purpose-designed one bearing the MG logo. The gearbox is already attached and the combined unit is fitted in the hull from the top, gearbox first, to be followed by the wheels, interior trim and hood.

Each car then enters a test facility, its engine is started, the gases analysed, any necessary corrections are made, and the brakes tested. Lastly, the bumpers and headlamp cowls are added and the car is given a 20 mile road test – which is 18 more than the MGBs used to have – that is intended to identify any minor problems. Once back at Cowley, the cars are polished and are then ready to be transported to a Rover Dealership and from there will be delivered to the customer.

So how has the MG RV8 been judged by the motoring press and potential customers? Some of the first members of the public to evaluate the car were three lucky readers of *Auto Express* magazine. One was Geoff Downs who, after driving the MG said, 'Before today I thought that it was an expensive gimmick, but having driven it I really would spend my money on it. The ride was much smoother that I thought. . . Part and parcel of the experience was that beautiful V8 rumble. . . My only criticism was the driving position. At 6 ft 2 in, I found my line of vision was at the top of the windscreen. Also, my left leg was too close to the steering wheel. But what the hell, it was thrilling.' Geoff's views were broadly shared by his companions.

Autocar & Motor published its first full road test on the RV8 in its issue of 16 June 1993. It pithily summed up the MG as: '*For* Strong engine, beautifully built, feels pleasantly quaint. *Against* Poor handling, unrefined and rather lumpen ride.'

The magazine attained a top speed of 136 mph, which was 1 mph greater than that claimed by Rover, but as far as performance was concerned, 'it feels fast. . . However, it was all we could do to coax it under 7 secs [to 60 mph] suggesting that the RV8 is merely very swift.' Handling and ride, inevitably, reflected the limitations of a 30-year-old

design. Petrol consumption was variable and the car achieved an overall figure of 20.2 mph. The brakes came in for praise although it was felt that an ABS system should have been fitted as standard. More positively, 'You quite simply cannot quibble with the way the RV8 is pieced together. The quality of the interior materials, especially the leather, is top drawer, while you'd have to look a long way indeed to find a paint finish better than that which adorned the test RV8.'

It summed up the car thus: 'Whether the RV8 is good value or not depends on how you perceive it. If you judge it simply on it capabilities, it is hard to justify the expense.

'Look at it as a piece of nostalgia which provides both a trip down memory lane plus decent performance and the £25,440 purchase price is easier to swallow.'

As predicted, the MG RV8 remained in production until 1995, by which time Rover had built 1,996 examples with the balance of four cars made up by numbered but pre-production vehicles.

However, despite the company's hopes for the model, a mere 324 were bought by British customers. But no less than 80 per cent of production, amounting to 1,581 cars, was exported to Japan. These were fitted with air conditioning with the inlet tracts replacing the spotlights in the front spoiler.

The balance of 91 cars are accounted for by sales to the following countries: Germany 59, Holland 21, of which two were Japanese specification, Belgium five, Australia four and France two. The last vehicle was built on 22 November 1995 and was the culmination of 266 cars produced in 1993, 821 in 1994 and 909 manufactured in the final year.

By the time that the RV8 ceased production, the MG name was riding high on the new and, above all, wholly British engineered mid engined MGF, launched at the 1995 Geneva Motor Show. The highly acclaimed Longbridge-built open two seater is powered by Rover's 1.8 litre K-series engine.

With BMW, which bought Rover in 1994, pledged to maintain the indigenous nature of its products, MG is destined to be one of a handful of British marques to survive into the 21st century. This is a tribute to the outstanding qualities of MG's founder and its post war custodian: Cecil Kimber and John Thornley did their work well.

Appendix □

The Clubs

There are two principal clubs for MGB owners. The older of the two is the MG Car Club, founded in 1930 and, until 1969, was run from the MG factory at Abingdon. The club has 112 autonomous centres which covers the whole country. In addition, there are 65 associate centres throughout the world, including 33 in America and even one in Japan! There are MGB, MGC and MGB V8 registers and the club, having RAC affiliation, runs all manner of competitive events, including hill climbs, rallies and sprints, while there are four MG race meetings a year on the UK's principal circuits. Concours events are also held and the one shown here took place over a weekend at Harewood, Yorkshire. Roy Pickard (left) proudly displays the Naylor Brothers Challenge Rose Bowl, which he won with his 1971 MGB GT. Alongside Roy is Alastair Naylor, of the MG T Type specialists, which sponsored the concours d'élegance. Owners of MG cars of any age are welcome to join. The address is MG Car Club, Kimber House, PO Box 251, Abingdon, Oxon OX14 1FF.

Like the MG Car Club, the MG Owners' Club, welcomes owners of all MGs. Only founded in 1973, its growth has been stupendous and currently, with about 45,000 members, is the largest one-make car club in the world. The club has 140 areas within 14 regions of the country, while there are further affiliates and areas in over 20 different countries throughout the world. The club operates its own insurance scheme with cars receiving full comprehensive cover and agreed valuation. Other benefits include free

technical advice on all MG cars. The club produces *Enjoying MG,* a monthly full colour magazine, which also includes *Enjoying MG News,* containing dates and reports of events in a member's local area, while *MG Mart* contains details of hundreds of MGs for sale each month. Each member also receives the Club's handbook which contains a listing of MG spares and restoration specialists. The photograph shows a gathering of MGBs at one of the club's recent events.

GDC 604L

MG Car Club president, John Thornley, inspects one of the then new LE MGBs at a club meeting in the spring of 1981.

Bottom left: Enthusiasm for MGBs is world wide, particularly in America, where the vast majority of Bs were exported. This is one of the largest gatherings in the US, with plenty of 'rubber'-bumpered cars in evidence.

Below: The MG Car Club's Abingdon headquarters, Kimber House, next to the former MG Administrative Block in Cemetery Road, which was at the start and finish of the factory's pre-war test route. A plaque on the front of the building commemorates its opening in July 1990 by Lord Montagu of Beaulieu. (Courtesy of MG Car Club)

A fine action shot of a chrome bumpered roadster, pictured at an MG Car Club meeting at Brands Hatch in 1975.

MGB
The illustrated history

Bottom left: The workshop facilities which are available to MG Owners' Club members where they can undertake body and mechanical repairs on their cars as well as servicing. (Courtesy MG Owners' Club)

Concours events are popular with MG Owners' Club members while the suitably adorned bus leaves members in little doubt about which club they belong to! (Courtesy MG Owners' Club)

The MG Owners' Club also organises race meetings for its members.

In 1988 there was a 15 round MGOC/BARC racing championship.

Appendix II

MGB
Modifications & Production figures

THERE HAVE BEEN thousands of modifications made to the MGB throughout its production life and it is obviously impossible to list them all. So what follows are the principal ones and, where appropriate, the chassis number at which the change was made.

But first a word about the code that precedes the numbers proper. At its announcement, the MGB roadster's chassis number prefix was G-HN3. G is the BMC letter for MG (B was BMC Industries, C Austin Healey, H Miscellaneous, J Commercial, M Morris, R Riley and W Wolseley). The second letter, H, relates to the engine's capacity from 1400 to 1999cc and thus the B Series unit. N indicates that the car is a tourer. When the GT arrived for 1966 with it came the D designation which replaced N where appropriate. 3 is the MG series number. This really harks back to the MGA 1500 which was Series 1, while 2 was the Mark 11 MGA of 1960. So the Mark 1 MGB of 1962, and it was only retrospectively described as such, was Series 3. The only *official* MGB mark number was 11 of 1968 which was designated a Series 4 car and the chassis number prefix was changed accordingly. For the 1970 model year came the Series 5 while MGBs for 1972 were referred to as Mark 111s in the contemporary motoring press. Finally L was introduced to indicate left-hand drive, and U was used on MGBs sold on the American market.

The start number of 101 is again a BMC influence, its having first been used on the 1951 Austin A30. Up until the phasing-out of the TD in 1954, MG chassis numbers began with 0251 which was the factory's telephone number. However, with the creation of BMC

in 1952, this long established tradition disappeared and the TF that succeeded the TD began with 501. The first MG model to begin with 101 was the MG Midget of 1961 though just to complicate matters the MGA's chassis numbers start at 10101! But the MGB reverted to 101. Also, from the 1970 model year, a suffix was introduced, A for 1970, B for 1971 and so on, though the letter I was avoided so cars for the 1978 model year have a J suffix.

The MGB, as already noted, went into production in May 1962, initially in roadster form, from chassis number G-HN3 101. The first alteration to this specification, announced in January 1963, was the option of overdrive. This was a D-type Laycock de Normanville unit, actuated by a facia-mounted switch. The 0.080:1 ratio reduced final drive in third and top gears from 5.37:1 and 3.92:1 to 4.31:1 and 3.14:1. The only other significant change for the year came with the arrival of a factory-approved hardtop in June. A closed-circuit crankcase breathing system was introduced in February 1965 at chassis number G-HN3 31021. At chassis number G-HN3 48766, the original three-bearing engine was replaced by a five-bearing unit. At the same time the oil cooler was standardised (it having been an option from the model's outset though had been a standard fitment on Export cars). Simultaneously the mechanical speedometer was replaced by an electronic unit and the fuel gauge's accuracy was improved. At March 1965 (G-HN3 56743) the fuel tank's capacity was increased from 10 to 12 gallons. Also the two-strap mounting arrangement was dispensed with and replaced by securing bolts. Subsequently (at

G-HN3 57986) the door handles were altered, the original pull-out types were dispensed with and push button ones introduced. This coincided with the locks and internal door mechanisms, being altered.

A closed version of the model, the MGB GT (from chassis number G-HD3 71933) was announced in October 1965 for the 1966 model year. In November 1966 a front anti-roll bar was fitted to the roadster (G-HN3 108039). The GT had employed a more robust Salisbury-type rear axle and this was introduced on the open car in April 1967. This changeover occurred at G-HN3 132923 on the wire-wheeled cars and at 139215 on the MGB's fitted with disc wheels.

The Mark 11 MGB was unveiled in October 1967 for 1968, so the chassis number prefix was changed to G-HN4 (for fourth series) 138401 on the roadster and G-HN4 139472 on the GT. Under-bonnet changes included the introduction of an alternator in place of a dynamo and thus a negative earth system, and a pre-engaged starter in place of the earlier Bendix type. The gearbox tunnel was enlarged to facilitate the fitting of automatic transmission while the all-synchromesh gearbox of the simultaneously announced MGC was fitted. MGBs for the American market began to differ from their European counterparts. Their engines were fitted with emission control equipment, along with dual circuit brakes and an energy absorbing steering column.

The MGC arrived for the 1968 season at chassis number G-CN 101 (roadster) while the GT began at G-CD 110. At chassis number 4236, during 1968, those cars fitted with overdrive had their rear axle ratios changed from 3.31:1 to 3.7:1 and non-overdrive models from 3.07:1 to 3.31:1. Other changes for 1969 included the fitting of a closer ratio gearbox, five-stud Rostyle wheels on those cars destined for export and reclining seats were standardised. The model was discontinued at chassis number G-CN 9099 in August 1969 (tourer) and G-CD 9102 (GT) in September.

The fifth series MGB arrived in October 1969 at chassis number G-HN5 187211 (roadster) and G-HD5 187841 (GT). These cars were fitted with a new, recessed radiator grille with a chrome surround and the MG badge lurking within (the Austin Healey Sprite/MG Midget's front end was

similarly altered). The fact that MG was part of the British Leyland Motor Corporation was indicated by the presence of small Leyland motifs mounted each side just forward of the doors, on each front wing. The bumper overriders on US cars were now fitted with rubber inserts while black and silver Rubery Owen Rostyle wheels were introduced though wires could be had at extra cost. The car's interior was also facelifted with new reclining seats, vinyl rather than leather finished, and a smaller steering wheel with three drilled spokes. Improvements for 1971, introduced in September 1970 (G-HN5-219001), included a new Michelotti designed hood. There were also telescopic engine and boot stays; when the boot was opened, on went an interior light. Ventilation and heating system was also improved.

The 'Mark 111' Bs, introduced in October 1971, saw yet more changes to the model's interior (G-HN5/G-HD5 258001). The place previously occupied on the dashboard by the radio now contained a pair of swivelling fresh air ducts, the radio being transferred to console below the dash. Rocker switches replaced tumblers. A new console, introduced between the front seats, also featured. A collapsible energy-absorbing steering column, a feature of American-sold MGBs from 1968, was extended to those Bs sold in non-US markets.

The MGBs radiator grille was again revised for 1973 in October 1972 (G-HN5 294251, G-HD5 296001). The famous octagon was again more prominent and the radiator grille had black mesh with a chrome surround. In came a leather-bound steering wheel with slotted spokes and a similarly upholstered matching gear lever knob. A cigar lighter was standardised while windscreen wipers were black finished rather than chrome.

The MGB GT V8 was introduced in August 1973 at chassis number G-D2D1 101 and continued in production until September 1976 (G-D2D1 2903).

In September 1973 (G-HN5/G-HD5-328101), the MGBs under-bonnet layout was made common with the V8. Radial tyres were standardised and the automatic gearbox option was withdrawn. Those cars sold in America were fitted with vertical rubber overriders. The biggest external change of all to the MGB came in September 1974 for the 1975 model year (G-HN5 360301 and

MGB
The illustrated history

G-HD5 361001 in the UK, and G-HD5 363082 for the US market) with the introduction of black polyurethane bumpers. The roadster's ride height was also increased, the GT having been withdrawn from the American market at the end of 1974. In addition, in came hazard warning lights, door mirrors and servo assisted brakes, the latter having been previously offered as an optional extra. The overdrive unit was changed to an LH type, the ratio being slightly lowered from 0.8021:1 to 0.82:1. At last the two six volt batteries, an MGA inheritance, were replaced by a single 12 volt unit. In June 1975, overdrive, another longstanding option was standardised at G-HN5 380278 and G-HD5 379495.

The front anti-roll bar was thickened-up in August 1976 (G-HN5 410001) and a rear bar standardised. Cars for 1977 again bene-

fited from a revamped interior. The instrument panel was redesigned along with the central console which received an electric clock. Seats were finished in cheerful deckchair type material and were fitted with head restraints. The overdrive switch which had hitherto resided on the facia was incorporated in the gear lever knob in the manner of contemporary Triumphs. There was a new four spoked steering wheel which was lower-geared, at three and a half rather than three turns lock to lock. The engine's cooling system was sealed with a separate catch tank. Petrol tank capacity was reduced from 12 to 11 gallons.

Further minor modifications included the fitting, from April 1977, of inertia reel seat belts, and, in January 1978, twin radio speakers were mounted in the doors. The last 1000 MGBs were completed in October 1980, the Limited Edition model, available in roadster and GT form (from chassis numbers G-HN5 522581 and G-HD5 522422). The final MGBs were built on 23 October, the roadster being G-HN5 523001 and GT G-HD5-523002.

MGB production 1962-1980

	Roadster			GT			
	Home	Export	Total	Home	Export	Total	Grand T.
1962	540	3 978	4 518				4 518
1963	3 020	20 288	23 308				23 308
1964	4 321	22 221	26 542				26 542
1965	4 742	19 437	24 179	350	174	524	24 703
1966	4 050	18 625	22 675	2 415	7 826	10 241	32 916
1967	2 749	12 379	15 128	5 276	6 120	11 396	26 524
1968	1 609	15 746	17 355	2 750	5 602	8 352	25 707
1969	2 288	16 762	19 050	3 274	8 938	12 212	31 262
1970	2 841	20 803	23 644	4 466	7 996	12 462	36 106
1971	3 046	19 398	22 444	5 311	6 799	12 110	34 554
1972	4 898	21 294	26 192	7 883	5 291	13 174	39 366
1973	3 034	16 531	19 565	5 760	4 458	10 218	29 783
1974	1 622	17 344	18 966	3 899	5 682	9 581	28 547
1975	1 118	18 848	19,966	4 122	487	4 609	24 575
1976	1 891	23 969	25 860	3 083	615	3 698	29 558
1977	2 262	22 228	24 490	4 065	126	4 191	28 681
1978	2 836	19 170	22 006	5 529	129	5 658	27 664
1979	921	18 976	19 897	3 346	127	3 473	23 370
1980	2 022	8 982	11 004	3 378	46	3 424	14 428
Total	49 810	336 979	386 789	64 907	60 416	125 323	512 112

From 1965 to 1968, Mk 1 and Mk 11 versions of Roadsters and GT models were available simultaneously.

MGC and MGB GT V8 production

	MGC Roadster	MGC GT	MGB GT V8*	Total	
1967	189	41		230	* The annual figures shown
1968	2566	2462		5028	throughout differ from those
1969	1787	1954		3741	mentioned in the text. This is due to
1972			3		different counting methods. However,
1973			1069		the 2591 total of V8s manufactured
1974			854		remains the same.
1975			489		
1976			176		
Total	4542	4457	2591	8999	

MG RV8 — Prototype and test vehicles

Veh id	Build ref	Reg no	Colour	Remarks
Development vehicles				
ZZ2841	ADDDEV01	U/R*	BMH Green	MGB uprated with 3.5 litre V8 engine, later 3.9 uprated suspension and brakes. Became styling vehicle.
ZZ2842	ADDDEV02	YWU 486S	Red	MGB uprated as above. Engine cooling test.
ZZ2843	ADDDEV03	UGT 808N	White	
ZZ2844	ADDDEV04	U/R	White	* Originally LFC 436S.
Validation vehicles				
ADD1	ADDVAL01	SFH 639W	Red	Rear axle test, misuse and abuse, stop/start transmission testing. MGB body.
ADD2	ADDVAL02	TAO 92W	Black	60,000 mile durability test. *Car* magazine assessment. MGB body.
ADD3	ADDVAL03	K638 WOK	Flame Red	First Adder built. Specification test car.
ADD4	ADDVAL04	K637 WOK	Nightfire	High-speed test car and electrical test.
ADD5	ADDVAL05	K377 CAC	BRG	Chassis test car, Longbridge.
ZZ2951	ADDVAL06	U/R	No paint	Body-in-white, body kit development.
ZZ2952	ADDVAL07	K140 CDU	Le Mans Green	Photographic car, MG RV8 brochure.
ZZ2954	ADDVAL09	U/R		Manufacturing.
ZZ2957	ADDVAL12	U/R	White Gold	
ZZ2958	ADDVAL13	K251 CDU	Le Mans Green	Customer viewing, dealer support, TV car *Peak Practice*.
ZZ2959	ADDVAL14	U/R	Le Mans Green	Motor Show car (NEC, Geneva, MG Day).
ADD101	ADD101	K139 CDU	Caribbean Blue	Specification testing, figure 8 and pave.
ADD201	ADD201	U/R	Caribbean Blue	Homologation car and service training.
ADD202	ADD202	K317 EHP	Nightfire	Brake testing.
ADD204	ADD204	U/R	Diamond White	Pave testing.
ZZ3883	ADD205	U/R	Diamond White	
ZZ3428	ADD301	K398 FDU	Woodcote Green	Durability car and team use.
	ADD302			Belfast Motor Show and dealer demonstration car.
	ADD303			Japan car, air conditioning test.
ZZ3884	ADD304	U/R	Diamond White	
ZZ4507	ADD401	K574 FKV	Black	18,000 mile durability test, then team demonstration.
ZZ4642	ADD402		Oxford Blue	
ZZ4630	ADD403		Old Eng White	
ZZ4643	ADD404		BRG	Australia
ZZ4644	ADD405		Oxford Blue	Dealer demonstration cars.
ZZ4645	ADD406		BRG	
ZZ4631	ADD407		Le Mans Green	
ZZ4632	ADD408		Nightfire	
ZZ4646	ADD501		Oxford Blue	
	ADD502			
	ADD503			Dealer demonstration cars
	ADD504			
ZZ4550	ADD505		Le Mans Green	
ZZ4651	ADD506		Le Mans Green	
ZZ4759	ADD507		Nightfire	
ZZ4653	ADD508		Nightfire Blue	Press cars
ZZ4694	ADD509		White Gold	

Appendix III

MG EX & BMC Project numbers

MG EX and BMC/Leyland ADO numbers of MGB and associated projects			

EX No.	ADO No.	Year produced	Remarks
135	–	1938	Goldie Gardner record breaker based on 1934 Magic Magnette
172	–	1951	Le Mans car for George Phillips, TD based
175	–	1952	Prototype MGA
179	–	1954	EX 175 based record car
181	–	1957	Mid engined record breaker
182	–	1955	Le Mans MGAs
183	–	1955	Tubular chassis MGA project for 1956 Le Mans
186	–	1956	Car based on above design
205	–	1957	MGA replacement with separate chassis
205/1	–	1957	Body based on EX 181 record breaker
205/2R	–	1957	Drawing made from Frua bodied MGH
214	23	1958	MGB, manufactured 1962/80
214/1	–	1958	MGB body quarter scale drawing
214/2	–	1958	Design study for V4 engine in 214 body
214/3	–	1958	Design study for MGA Twin Cam engine in 214 body
214/4	–	1958	Design study for 4 cyl C Series engine in 214 body
214/5	–	1958	Variation on above
214/6/7/8	–	1958	Variations on V4 theme
216	–	1958	Design study for V4 engine in MGA
–	34	–	Mini based MG sports car project, cancelled 1960
–	17	1963/75	Austin 1800
227	–	1965/80	MGB GT
235	–	1964	Competition MGB
–	51	–	Austin Healey version of MGC, cancelled 1966
–	52	1967/69	MGC
241	–	1968	Competition MGC
–	68	1969	Condor project, mock up only
–	21	1969	Maxi powered mid engined car, mock up only
249	–	1973/6	MGB GT V8
250	–	1972	MGB safety car for US exhibition
–	28	1971/80	Morris Marina
–	76	1974/80	Rubber bumpered MGB/V8

Index

Those page numbers in **bold** *type refer to illustrations*

Bibliography

The MG Story . . . from First to Last, BL Heritage,
    1981
MG The Art of Abingdon by John McLellan, Motor
    Racing Publications, 1982
John McLellan, Motor Racing Publications, 1982
MG by McComb, Osprey, 1978.
MGB by F. Wilson McComb, Osprey Auto History,
    1982.
MGB Super Profile by Lindsay Porter, Haynes, 1982.
Guide to Purchase and DIY Restoration of the MGB
    by Lindsay Porter, Haynes, 1982.
The MGA, MGB and MGC, a Collector's Guide, by
    Graham Robson, Motor Racing Publications, 1978.
The Mighty MGs by Graham Robson, David and
    Charles, 1982.
Safety Fast by John Thornley, Motor Racing
    Publications, 1956.

Magazines

Autocar
Autocar & Motor
Motor
Classic Cars
Classic and Sportscar
Enjoying MG
Safety Fast
MG Magazine, 'Sydney Enever, Mr MG', 1988

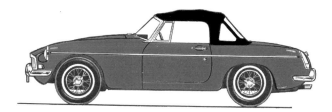

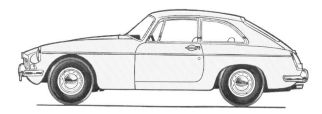

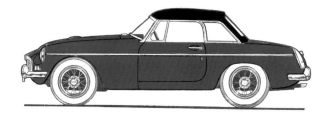
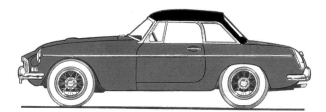
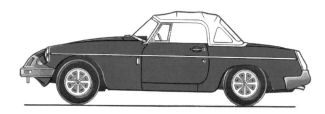
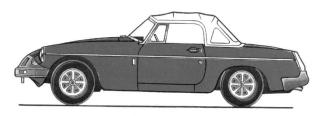
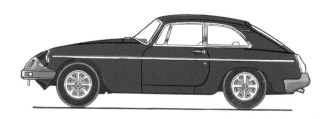
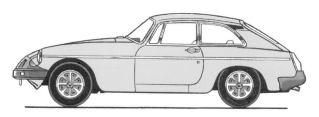